THE USE
OF COLOR
IN INTERIORS

SECOND EDITION

Albert O. Halse

McGRAW-HILL BOOK COMPANY
New York   St. Louis   San Francisco   Auckland
Bogotá   Düsseldorf   Johannesburg   London
Madrid   Mexico   Montreal   New Delhi
Panama   Paris   São Paulo   Tokyo
Singapore   Sydney   Toronto

Library of Congress Cataloging in Publication Data

Halse, Albert O, date.
    The use of color in interiors.

    Bibliography: p.
    Includes index.
1.   Color in interior decoration.   I.   Title.
NK2115.5.C6H34   1978   747   77-14472
ISBN 0-07-025624-1

34567890 HDHD 898765432

*The editors for this book were Jeremy Robinson and Joan Zseleczky,
the designer was Naomi Auerbach, and the production supervisor
was Teresa F. Leaden. It was set in Optima Medium
by Monotype Composition Company, Inc.*

Printed and bound by Halliday Lithograph.

CONTENTS

chapter five FACTORS CONTRIBUTING TO CONTEMPORARY COLOR USAGE 45

chapter six THE APPLICATION OF COLOR: BUILT-IN MATERIALS 67

chapter seven THE APPLICATION OF COLOR: FURNITURE 113

chapter eight THE APPLICATION OF COLOR: FURNISHINGS 131

COLOR PLATES

PREFACE

Color is a very important part of our lives. We are surrounded by it; we communicate with it; we select our clothes, automobiles, houses, paintings, and even food packages by it. It is used to make us happy, to make us hungry, to promote serenity, and to encourage piety. It invites us into one architectural space and drives us out of another.

This book was written to explain the reasons behind the selection of colors for interior spaces. Each color selection must include the proper consideration of all contributing factors. A number of excellent books have been written on the history, chemistry, and psychology of color. Much has also been written about color for merchandising. Individual books on furniture, fabrics, carpets, and the decorative arts are readily available, as are a variety of color notation systems. Magazines devoted to architecture, interior design, and homemaking often feature articles or entire issues on one of the many aspects of color for interiors. Question-and-answer columns in newspapers frequently deal with the use of color, and the subject is often discussed on radio and television.

This book provides an overview of the various aspects of color as it is applied to the design of interior spaces. A discussion of the various color systems and their use enables readers to experiment with these systems to whatever extent they wish. The book also provides useful technical information, such as the relationship between color and artificial light, as well as information about the psychological aspects of the uses of color.

The reader is introduced to the relationships between color and environment, specifically in regard to built-in materials, furniture, and furnishings. A short history of the use of color in interiors is presented so that readers will understand present-day uses of color in terms of the past and recognize that they must be part of the change that occurs around them. Technological and sociological background is provided for the same reason.

In short, the reader is given the opportunity to look behind the scenes in order to understand the factors governing the professional selection of color schemes. Architecture and interior design change, and color usage also changes. Each color problem is unique; its successful solution depends upon a proper analysis of the factors involved. An understanding of the underlying principles that govern the use of color in interior design will enable the reader to adapt to new situations as they arise.

Albert O. Halse

ACKNOWLEDGMENTS

This book was to a great extent made possible by the cooperation of architects, interior designers, and those engaged in the manufacture and supply of those items which are used in the design of interior architectural spaces. To all who gave freely of their time and information I offer my gratitude. I also appreciate the material loaned to me by many individual companies, societies, and associations. My sincere apologies are extended to those whose names I may have omitted, because of space considerations, when discussing individual materials. I also wish to thank the many persons who loaned photographs to me; to those whose photographs could not be included, also because of insufficient space, I offer my apologies. Last, I wish to thank my secretary and research assistant, Helen Ahnemann, for her many contributions to the project.

American Carpet Institute (integrated with
    Carpet Cushion Council, Dalton, GA)

American Olean Tile Company
Lansdale, PA
    Louis D. Methfessel

Amtico Flooring Division
American Biltrite, Inc.
Trenton, NJ

Armstrong Cork Company
Lancaster, PA

Benjamin, Robert
New York, NY

Belgian Linen Association
New York, NY
    Durawall, Inc., New York, NY

Bergen Bluestone Company, Inc.
Paramus, NJ
    Rod Fitzpatrick

Bigelow Sanford, Inc.
Greenville, S.C.
    Joyce Lambert, Public Relations Consultant

Louis W. Bowen
New York, NY

Champion International Building Products
    Division
Stamford, CT
    Martha Nold, Public Relations

John D'Amico, Architect
Waterbury, CT

DuPont Company
New York, NY
    Judith Mortenson, Public Relations

Duro-Test Corporation
North Bergen, NJ
    Lawrence H. Johnson, Vice President,
        Advertising and Public Relations
    Luke Thorington, Vice President, Engineering

Edward Fields, Inc.
New York, NY

Fine Hardwoods and American Walnut
    Association
Chicago, IL

Finneran & Haley, Inc.
Ardmore, PA
    Lorraine L. Coalson, Architectural Consultant

Formica Corporation
Cincinnati, OH

GAF Corporation
Floor Products, New York, NY
    Sylvia K. Low, Senior Publicist

General Electric, Lamp Marketing Dept.
    Nancy E. Christensen, Specialist, Residential Lighting
    George E. Matilo, Manager, Electric
        Utility Relations

Gracie, Charles R. & Sons, Inc.
New York, NY

Greeff Fabrics, Inc.
New York, NY

Hardwood Plywood Manufacturers Association
Arlington, VA

Harper & George, Inc.
New York, NY

Harris Manufacturing Company
Johnson City, TN
 C. Warner Tweed, Sales Manager

Boris Kroll, Inc.
New York, NY
 Marjorie F. Kronengold, Design Coordinator

Levolor-Lorentzen, Inc.
Hoboken, NJ
 C. P. Scott, Regional Manager

Marshall, William L., Ltd.
New York, NY

John Mielach Company, Woodworking
Edison, NJ

Benjamin Moore & Company
Montvale, NJ
 Lee C. McAlister, Senior Vice President
 and Vice President, Marketing

Munsell Color
Baltimore, MD
 Louise P. Galyon, Resident Manager

National Association of Mirror
 Manufacturers
Washington, DC

National Terrazzo & Mosaic Association,
 Inc.
Alexandria, VA

William Pahlmann Associates, Inc.
New York, NY

PPG Industries, Inc.
Pittsburgh, PA
 Bonnie Bender, Manager, Color Marketing
 Anne Cain, Public Relations

E. Schenk, Architectural Representative

Scalamandre Wallpaper, Inc.
New York, NY

F. Schumacher & Co.
New York, NY

Selig Manufacturing Company, Inc.
Leominster, MA
 Elroy Edson, A.S.I.D., Designer
 Carole Frankel, Public Relations

The Martin-Senour Company
Bala Cynwyd, PA

Steelcase, Inc.
Grand Rapids, MI

Tile Council of America, Inc.
Princeton, NJ
 Lis King, Public Relations

3M Company
St. Paul, MN
 Lee Horn

Tropicraft
San Francisco, CA
 James E. McCloskey, President

Vicrtex Sales Division
L. E. Carpenter & Company
New York, NY

Wilson Art Brand Laminated Plastic
Temple, TX

Window Modes
New York, NY

Window Shade Manufacturers Association
New York, NY
 Hilda D. Sachs
 Cynthia Richter

The Wool Bureau, Inc.
New York, NY
 David Singer Associates
 New York, NY

chapter one

COLOR
THEORY AND
COLOR DESIGN

COLOR AND LIGHT

Many theories have been advanced to explain color. The illuminating Engineering Society's *IES Lighting Handbook* says: "Color is considered to be a mental phenomenon which is evoked by light striking the back of the eye after passing through the ocular media." Most authorities agree that objects themselves do not have color, but that the color of an object is determined by its relative ability to absorb light rays. Because objects do not absorb the same quantity of light at each wavelength, different colors are produced. When light strikes an object, it penetrates the surface somewhat. The extent of penetration and absorption depends upon the texture of the object. If an object absorbs all colors except red, red rays are reflected to the eye, and we call the object red. White light is a mixture of all colors. These colors may be seen when sunlight striking the curved surfaces of raindrops is spread into a rainbow. The same effect may be obtained by passing a narrow beam of light through a glass prism (see Figure 1.1).

White surfaces reflect all colors, absorbing none. Black surfaces, on the other hand, do not reflect colors, but absorb them. Thus black is the complete lack of light and color.

These basic facts are only a small part of the body of fascinating information about color and light amassed by scientists. But even in the world of science, different aspects of color concern different disciplines. For instance, the chemist may identify a color by a curved ink line produced by a spectrophotometer;

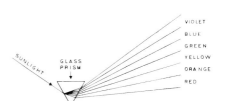

FIG. 1.1 *Refraction of light through a glass prism*

1

the physicist might add to the curved ink line another curve corresponding to certain aspects of the light source (that sends out energy which is then reflected off the sample); and the colorimetrist may take into account the relation between the visual response of a standard observer and the so-called stimulus aspects of the object.[1]

The psychologist, the artist, the architect, and the interior designer believe that certain other aspects of color must be considered. The appearance of color for them depends on viewing conditions, the surrounding objects or areas, the sizes and relative positions of objects, and the adaptive state of the viewer. It is for these reasons that for the purpose of this discussion we shall consider color as not merely reflection, but as an entity in itself, with its own properties.

Properties of Color

Color may be described as having three outstanding properties: hue, value, and intensity. Hue is the name of the color, such as blue, which differentiates it from another color, such as green. Value designates the brightness of a color, that is, whether the color is light or dark. Intensity, or chroma, denotes the extent to which the hue is free from any white constituent. The "temperature" of a color has no physical basis, but blue greens and blue violets, which seem to recede, are called "cool" colors; and reds, red oranges, and red violets, which seem to advance, are called "warm" colors.

Effects of Types of Light

Since color may be thought of as reflected light, the kind of light that falls upon an object will affect the object's apparent color. A color that appears to be bluish green in daylight will look yellowish green in incandescent light. Under daylight fluorescent lighting—which does not contain all the colors of the spectrum—the same color will appear to be completely blue. As the reader will see in Chapter 2, colors must be selected in the same kind of light as that in which they are to be used.

Effects of Surroundings on Colors

Certain other phenomena should be kept in mind when selecting colors for an interior space. There must be, for instance, a delicate balance between the several colors used: one color must predominate. A wall painted in a bright color will seem to be larger than it actually is, because a bright color is more stimulating to the retina than a grayed hue. A white area surrounded by a darker area appears to swell in dimension. If the same color is used in several parts of an architectural space, it may appear to be different in hue in different places because of the variation in the amount of light to which it is exposed and also because of the proximity of the other colors. An area painted yellow will seem larger than one painted orange, and an orange area will seem larger than one painted red. Invariably, a blue area will seem larger than a black one. A bright yellow pillow will not look the same on a cool gray sofa as it will on

[1] R. W. Burnham, R. M. Hanes, and C. J. Bartelson, *Color: A Guide to Basic Facts and Concepts,* New York: John Wiley & Sons, Inc., 1963, p. 2.

a tan one. The fabric of a chair will seem to change if it is moved from one background color to another. In short, colors affect one another. Used by itself, a color will often seem adequate in a given location, but when used near another color—even one of the same color family—it will suddenly appear to be "dirty." A yellowish green, for instance, can make certain shades of blue look purple when they are used together. A very dark shade of, say, mulberry used on a wainscot will make a very pale shade of the same color used on the upper wall appear white.

The fact that colors look different in different surroundings has led to many disappointments when colors have been selected for decoration with no thought of their eventual neighboring colors. Many a beautiful vase has been purchased because it looked magnificent in a carefully prepared store display, only to become just another item when placed in incompatible surroundings in the home. This phenomenon is also responsible for the fact that people can be disappointed in clothing they have bought: in a store, clothes are displayed under ideal conditions.

In interior design, colors of deep value, such as deep violet (in the chromatic circle, Plate 2), will seem to be heavier than pale colors, such as yellow. These deep colors can cause an imbalance in a room if too much of the deep color is used on one side or in one area. Finally, it should be remembered that light colors, or tints, always look brighter if they are viewed against a dark background, while dark hues usually seem more dramatic against a white background.

If a room is painted with one of the cool colors, the apparent size of the room will be increased. If one of the warm colors is used, the room will seem to be smaller. Bright colors such as yellow oranges, yellows, and yellow greens have a luminous quality and should be used to lighten an otherwise dark room.

Chromatic Circles and Solids

As science developed, an increasing amount of attention was given to the secrets of color. Robert Boyle discovered in the seventeenth century that red, yellow, and blue come from white light by reflection and refraction. Sir Isaac Newton, while trying to solve the problems of the telescope in 1666, noticed the refraction and dispersion of light through a prism. He discovered that all color is contained in sunlight and that when a beam of light passes through a prism, the direction of the light waves is changed (the violet waves, for example, are bent more sharply than red), and a rainbow results. Having obtained this information, Newton then formed the first chromatic circle by bending this sequence of colors, pulling the red and violet ends around, and joining the ends with purple. Johann Wolfgang von Goethe (1749–1832), the German poet, also dabbled in color and produced his own color wheel (Figure 1.2).

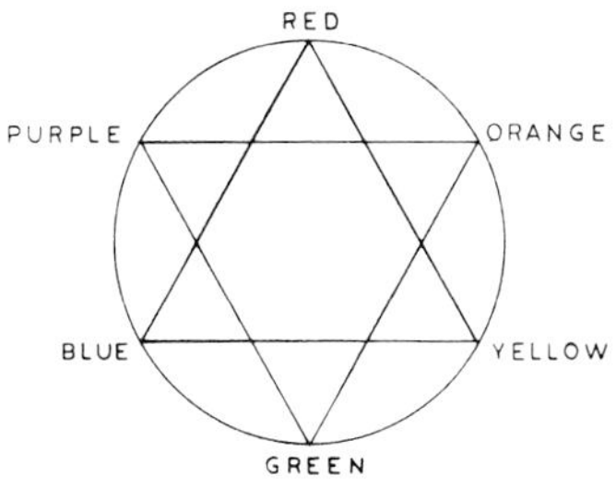

FIG. 1.2 Goethe's color wheel

COLOR SYSTEMS

There are in general use today several systems of color arrangement which can be employed according to the particular needs of the situation.[2] The uses of

[2] Ibid.

FIG. 1.3   The Ostwald color solid

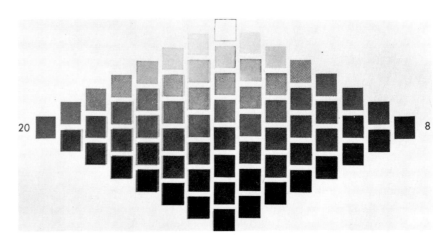

FIG. 1.4   Vertical section through the Ostwald color solid

the systems vary depending upon the basic plan of organization. One general plan for constructing a color system is the colorant mixture plan, based on a systematic mixture of pigments or dyes. In this plan a limited number of pigments or dyes is used to develop the colors in systematically varied proportions. Such systems have been developed by paint companies such as Martin-Senour, Pittsburgh, and Benjamin Moore, and these are discussed in Chapter 6 in the section on paint. The Plochere Color System is also a colorant mixture system.

A second general plan for constructing systems of object-color standards is called a Stimulus Synthesis Plan, of which the Ostwald system is an example. The system concerns itself with hue and with black and white. The Ostwald solid (Figure 1.3) is in the form of a double cone rather than a sphere. In this system there are twenty-four hues around the equator and eight value steps—from white at the top (or north pole) to black at the bottom (or south pole).

If the solid were cut in half vertically, the resulting section would be diamond-shaped, as in Figure 1.4. Each side (left and right) of the diamond would form a triangle. All the colors in the left one would, for instance, be derived from hue 20 (green), and those in the right triangle from hue 8 (red). Hues 20 and 8 are complements, since they appear opposite each other on the hue circle. The entire solid is, of course, made up of twelve sections such as this.

Since each section is made up of fifty-six colors, the complete solid contains 672 chromatic colors, plus the eight steps of the gray scale. In each color triangle, those vertical scales parallel to black and white (the isochromes) are equal in purity. Those colors parallel to a line between pure color and white (the isotones) in the top portion of the cone contain an equal amount of black. Those scales parallel to a line between pure color and black (the isotints in the bottom) have equal white content. Thus the Ostwald system is based upon the assumption that all colors may be mixed from combinations of pure hue, white, and black.

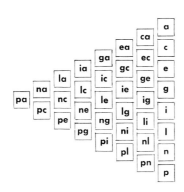

FIG. 1.5 One-half of the vertical section through the Ostwald color solid, showing the color notation

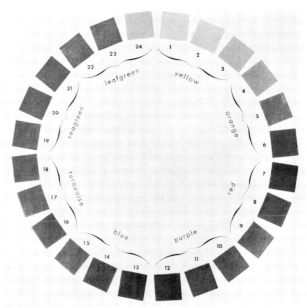

FIG. 1.6 Hues around the equator of the Ostwald color solid

The Ostwald Notation

Combinations of various numbers and letters make up the Ostwald color notations (see Figure 1.5). The hues, all full colors (free of white and black) and numbered from 1 to 24, are arranged in groups of three. These groups are respectively called yellow, orange, red, purple, blue, turquoise, sea green, and leaf green (Figure 1.6). The gray scale (see Figure 1.7) is lettered from A for white at the top to P for black at the bottom. Two of these letters are always required (see Figure 1.5): the first indicates that the color contains the same amount of white as the gray of the gray scale in which the series ends. The second letter indicates that the color contains the same amount of black as the gray of the gray scale in which the series ends. In other words, any two *letters* will specify the amount of white and black of a color in terms of the gray scale. Any *number* from 1 to 24 specifies hue; it is written at the beginning of the notation, like this: 22 PA.

The Ostwald color solid may be used for the selection of color harmonies. These are located according to geometric relationships within the various parts of the solid itself.[3]

Another general plan for constructing systems of object-color standards is called the Appearance Plan, in which color intervals are judged according to scales. The intervals between hues in an appearance system are determined by trained observers who judge the size of the intervals.[4] The Munsell color system, which falls into this category, was developed from judgments based on hue, value (brightness), and chroma.

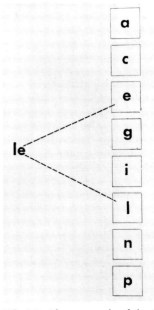

FIG. 1.7 The gray scale of the Ostwald color solid

[3] Egbert Jacobson, *Basic Color: An Interpretation of the Ostwald Color System,* Chicago: Paul Theobold & Company, 1948, Part II, pp. 56–108.

[4] Ibid., p. 168.

The Munsell System of Color

One of the best-known and widely respected systems of color standardization used in the United States today is that developed by Albert H. Munsell. He became greatly interested in the practical application of color and was disturbed by the fact that the popular names for colors did not describe them adequately for professional purposes. They are named after flowers or plants, such as violet, indigo, old rose, primrose; after fruits, such as peach, pomegranate, grape, avocado, plum; after places, such as french blue, naples yellow, or prussian blue; or after persons, such as Davy's gray or Hooker's green.*

Essentially the system consists of an orderly arrangement of colors in the shape of a three-dimensional color solid (see Plate 1). The system is based on a color circle of ten major hues made up of five principal hues, red, yellow, green, blue, and purple, and five intermediate hues, yellow-red, green-yellow, blue-green, purple-blue, and red-purple (see hue circle, Plate 1). Each hue is indicated by a symbol as follows:

Red	R	Yellow-Red	YR
Yellow	Y	Green-Yellow	GY
Green	G	Blue-Green	BG
Blue	B	Purple-Blue	PB
Purple	P	Red-Purple	RP

Each of the above major hues has been given a value of 5 in the inner scale around the hue circle (see Figure 1.8, hue symbols), i.e., 5 R, 5 YR, 5 Y, 5 GY, 5 G, 5 BG, 5 B, 5 PB, 5 P, and 5 RP. Between each of the major hues are values of 2.5, 10, and 7.5 for rough indication of hue. The outer scale of the hue circuit is divided into 100 equal segments to provide greater accuracy for indicating hue where needed.

In the Munsell color tree (Plate 1) each hue (H) is allotted ten segments of the hue circle, making 100 hues, and these hues form the horizontal center, or equator, of the color solid. The center segment of each color is considered the true color, and the remaining segments in each hue section vary according to their proximity to adjoining colors; for example, as red gets closer to yellow it contains more yellow, and this is indicated by the numerical designation.

The value (V) notation denotes the lightness or darkness of a hue, which is determined by a neutral core at the center of the hue circle. The core contains ten gradations from a supposedly perfect white (one having 100 percent reflectance) at the top to 0, a perfect black (having 0 percent reflectance) at the bottom.

The chroma (C) notation indicates the saturation of the hue, or the strength of the color. The chroma scale extends outward from the central core or axis, and the increments vary from 0 at a neutral gray to as high as 16, according to the amount of saturation produced by a given hue at a given value level. Since colors vary in chroma, or saturation, some colors extend farther from the neutral axis than others, and the solid is therefore not symmetrical. Pure red,

*As Munsell has said: "Can we imagine musical tones called lark, canary, crow, cat, dog, or mouse, because they bear some distant resemblance to the cries of those animals?"

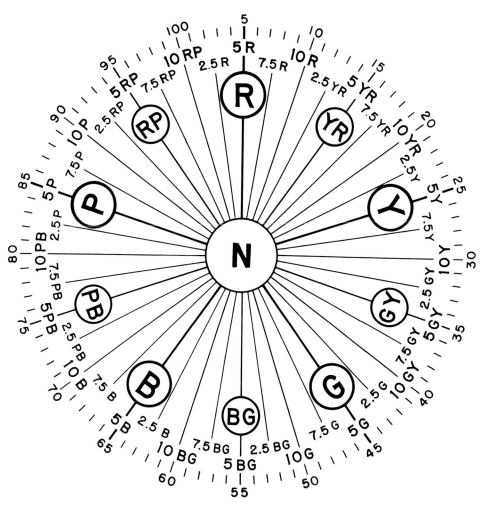

FIG. 1.8 Munsell hue symbols and their relation to one another
Munsell Color, Baltimore

with a chroma of 14, for instance, extends farther than blue-green, with a chroma of only 6 (see Figures 1.9 and 1.10).

A Munsell notation indicating hue, value, and chroma (H V/C) might be given as follows:[5]

| Vermilion | 5R 5/14 |
| Rose | 5R 5/4 |

With this information it is possible to describe exactly any given hue and to locate its place in the color solid. Furthermore, as Munsell stated,[6] one can "select one familiar color, and study what others will combine with it to please the eye," by the use of three typical paths: one vertical, with rapid change of value; another lateral, with rapid change of hue; and a third, inward, through the neutral center, to seek out the opposite color field. All other paths are combined by two or three of these typical directions in the color solid.

In addition to providing an excellent picture of color relationships in these

[5] Booklet, Munsell Color, Macbeth Division of Kollmorgen Corporation, Baltimore, MD 21218.

[6] A. H. Munsell, A Color Notation, 2d ed., Boston: George H. Ellis Co., 1907, p. 10.

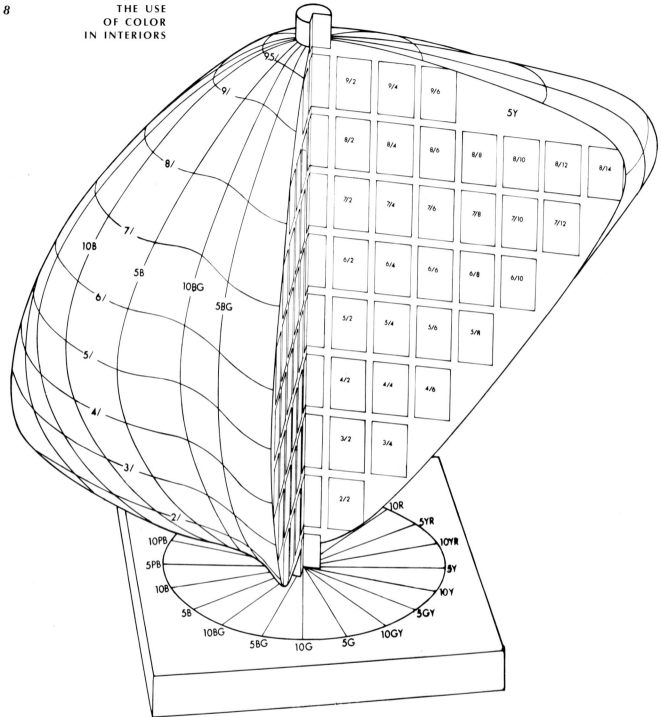

FIG. 1.9 Munsell color solid cut away to show constant hue 5y
Munsell Color, Baltimore

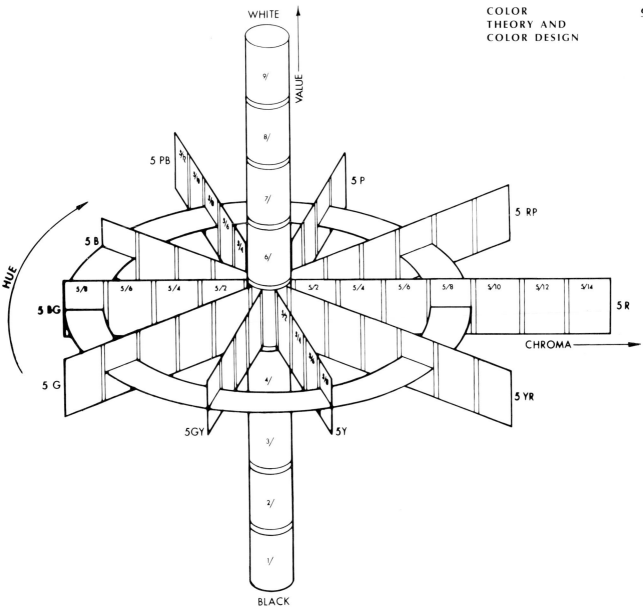

FIG. 1.10 Munsell hue, value, and chroma scales in color space
Munsell Color, Baltimore

dimensions, the Munsell "color tree" provides a splendid methodical way of standardizing, categorizing, and identifying colors. *The Munsell Book of Color,* which provides an orderly array of color reference samples representing the Munsell three-dimensional color system, is now accepted by the American National Standards Institute as a reference for the identification of color. It is widely used by industrial, commerical, and professional organizations.

The *Munsell Book of Color* is offered in a collection of 1488 glossy color chips or 1277 mat-finish color chips. Many other color tools are available from Munsell for various jobs concerned with color, including teaching and testing situations—e.g. the ANSI Safety Color Standards (see the section "Safety Color Guides" in Chapter 3). The Munsell system is accepted and used in many parts of the world.

Additional Research

Since 1915, when the first complete *Munsell Atlas of Color* was published, many avenues of research have been followed to improve the system. Studies made in cooperation with the National Bureau of Standards produced an improved edition of the *Munsell Book of Color* in 1929.

Other research in the early 1940s by a subcommittee of the Optical Society of America recommended changes in the color spacing to approach Munsell's ideal for equal visual steps. The International Commission on Illumination (Commission Internationale d'Éclairage), or CIE as it is generally referred to, has attained great importance in science with the "Standard Valency System," or CIE System, which permits mathematical definition of all manifestations of color.[7] The Munsell-CIE correlation provides the means for converting instrumental measurement data to Munsell notation and enables Munsell color standards to be produced to conform to psychophysical specifications. With the exception of a few colors, all Munsell color standards are produced to conform to Optical Society of America specifications within Munsell AAA tolerance. Colorants employed are the most stable available for the purpose. While it may not be economically feasible to produce color standards to match every conceivable color, custom color standards can be produced to order when necessary.

Research on color systems continues on many fronts, in diverse disciplines, and in various fields of manufacture. As new products are developed, new colorants are developed for them. It appears to be a never-ending cycle.

Other Color Systems

It is interesting to note that various groups of color investigators have adopted different color names: biologists use one set of terms, horticulturists another, and manufacturers of molded urea plastics and polystyrene plastics still another. Geologists do not use the color names for their rock-color charts that postage-stamp collectors use for their stamps. The architect and interior designer are probably most affected by Federal Specification TT-C-595 for Ready-mixed Paints and the color cards of the Textile Color Card Association of the United States, which use different names to describe their colors.

Other color systems in use today include:
Maerz & Paul, *Dictionary of Color*
Plochere Color System
Ridgway, *Color Standards and Color Nomenclature*
Taylor, Knoche, and Granville, *Descriptive Color Names Dictionary*
U. S. Government branches
　　Department of Agriculture

[7] Harald Küppers, *Color: Origin, Systems, Uses*, New York: Van Nostrand Reinhold, 1973, p. 106.

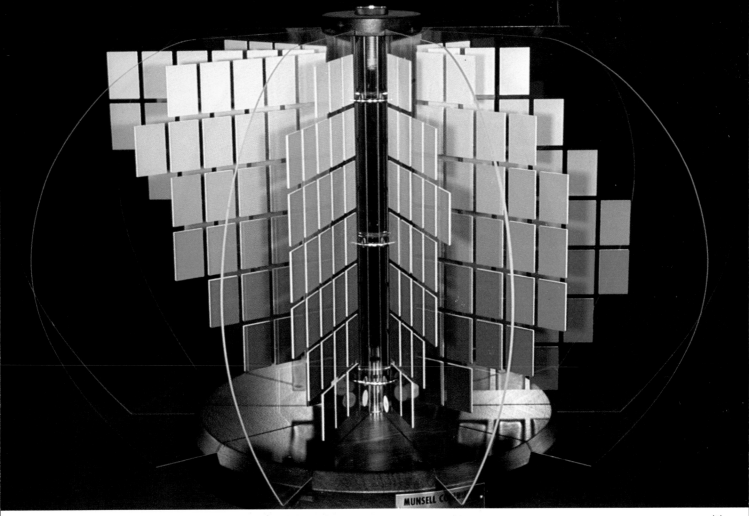

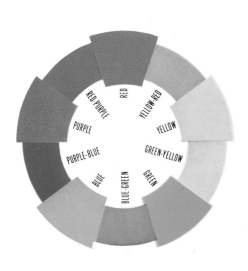

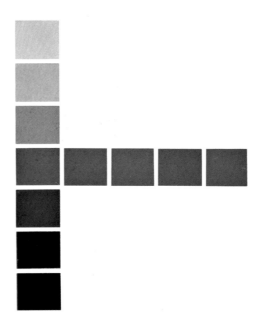

1. (a) Munsell color tree
   (b) Munsell vivid chromatic colors in circle
   (c) Value-chroma order

Munsell Color, Baltimore, MD

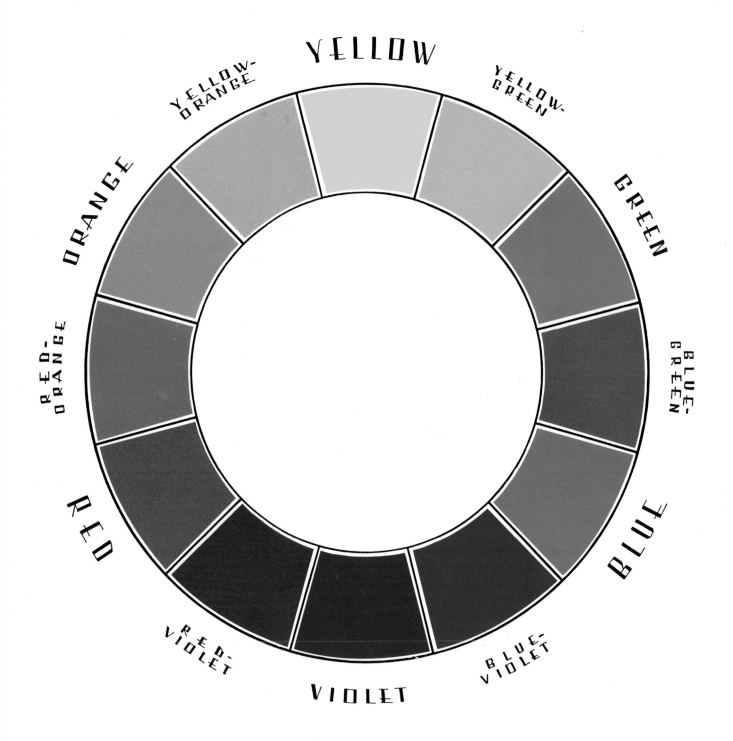

2. Twelve-hue chromatic circle

Army
Navy
Ordnance
Forest Service
Marine Corps
General Services Administration (Public Buildings Service)

Some color systems in use combine characteristics of the general plans described earlier.

Universal Color Language

The Inter-Society Color Council (ISCC), founded in 1931, consists of delegates from twenty societies of national scope as well as other individual members who are interested in various aspects of color. From their work over many years in cooperation with the United States Government National Bureau of Standards (NBS), there was published in 1955 the ISCC-NBS *Color Names Dictionary*. Through the years this work has continued, as the need for some means to correlate and standardize the specification of color has been deemed of great importance. In 1965[8] their efforts resulted in the publication of the Universal Color Language by Kenneth L. Kelly, physicist with the National Bureau of Standards, who has worked for many years on the development and extension of the ISCC-NBS Method of Designating Colors and *Dictionary of Color Names*.

The UNIVERSAL COLOR LANGUAGE is based upon a hue circle containing five generic *Centroid Colors:*.

Red   Blue
Yellow   Purple
Green

The latest edition of *Color Universal Language* and *Dictionary of Names*[9] to further aid in the specification of color has as its aims the following:

1. To be understood by the public, at least in a general way

2. To describe a color with different degrees of accuracy

3. To use color names or numeral/letter designations interchangeably

4. To specify color tolerances around a standard color

5. To describe the color in terms of the best known color-order systems or collections of color samples

6. To describe with the even greater accuracies that will be demanded in the future

7. To correlate visual descriptions with instrumental measurements of a color

8. To provide meaningful translation of exotic or promotional color names

The Universal Color Language includes six levels of fineness of color designation:

Level 1 (least precise)   Designated by color name

[8] Alexander F. Styne, ASID, IDSA, *The Universal Color Language—A Working Tool for the Designer, CS,* May 1976.

[9] Published by U. S. Department of Commerce, National Bureau of Standards, NBS Special Publication 440, December 1976.

Level 2	Designated by color name
Level 3	Designated by color name
Level 4	Designated by numeral and/or letter
Level 5	Designated by numeral and/or letter
Level 6 (most precise)	Designated by numeral and/or letter

Level 5 is illustrated by Munsell notation. Since the spacing of the samples in the *Munsell Book of Color* is nearly uniform, it is possible through comparison of a color with the Munsell standard scales of hue, value, and chroma to make a comparison. An experienced observer can with reasonable accuracy make such a comparison.

As increasing accuracy is required and more sophisticated measuring equipment becomes available, Level 7 will be developed.

The Universal Color Language, consisting of the Centroid Colors aforementioned and the above-noted levels of accuracy, contains also *The Color Names Dictionary (CND)* and several other divisions. This dictionary records about 7500 color names, all annotated so that it is possible to translate one color vocabulary into another and relate color names to the Munsell system. It is possible, by means of an intricate system of organization and notation, to use the dictionary in many different ways. Under the heading "Beige" (page 88) we find three listings, plus over a dozen "beiges" with modifiers, such as beige-light, beige-mode, beige-rose, and beige-yellow.

One ISCC-NBS designation for "Beige" is l. gy. y Br 79 (79. l. gy. y Br). If we check Section 14 of *Dictionary of Color Names*, we find a heading:

79. Light Grayish Yellowish Brown

Under Section 13, Color Name Charts, we find that the Munsell Notation for this color is 9.7 YR 6.4/2.5. Under the general heading "79. Light Grayish Yellowish Brown" in *Dictionary of Color Names*, p. 51, we find the following:

Maerz and Paul

Almond (Brown)	13B6	Nougat	13A5
Atmosphere	12A3	Nude	11A4
Belleek	11B3	Pawnee	13B6
Biarritz	13B3	Pecan	13B5
Biscuit	13B6	Seasan	11A4
Bronze Clair	13D2		
Burlwood	13A5	Plochere	
Champagne	11B3	Gravel	189 0 6-e
Cobweb	5B7	Smog	188 0 6-d
Cuban Sand	13A3		
Doe	13B6	Ridgway	
Elmwood	13B3	Avellaneous	XL 17'''b
Folkstone	13A3	Drab	XLVI 17''''
Grain	13B5	Drab-Gray	XLVI 17''''d
Gravel	13A4	Light Drab	XLVI 17''''b
Mauve Blush	12A3	Wood Brown	XL 17'''
Mavis	13B5		
Meerchaum	13A4	Taylor, Knoch, Granville	
Miami Sand	13B3	Beige m	3 ge

Bisque gm	3 ec	Buff	S
Camel m	3 ge	Dull Yellowish Brown	A
Light Beige gm	3 ec	Fumosus	B
		Gray Bistre	S
Textile Color Card Association		Griseo-Sepiaceus	B
Ecru	70103	Light Brownish Gray	SC
Nude	70139	Light Gray	SC
		Orange Brown	S
Other Sources		Pale Brown	SC
Avellaneus	B	Pale Yellowish Brown	RC
Bistre	S	Very Pale Brown	SC
Brown	S	Vinoso-Bubalinus	B
Brown Bistre	S		

Key

B   Color Terminology in Biology

S   Postage-Stamp Color Names, William H. Beck

A   American Association of Textile Chemists and Colorists and Society of Dyers and Colourists

SC   U.S. Department of Agriculture Soil Color Charts

RC   National Research Council, Rock-Color Chart

Also available from the National Bureau of Standards is the NBS Standard Sample No. 2106, ISCC-NBS Centroid Color Charts. The colors are in the form of one-inch square glossy paint-on-paper, fastened to a variable gray background. The color chip for 79. l. gy. y Br is shown, with other colors, on a sheet entitled "Orange Yellow Yellowish Brown."

The Chromatic Circle and Its Use

The work of the architect and the interior designer, by and large, is done with products which are the end results of the research and manufacturing techniques of others. While there are instances when architects or interior designers will be called upon to specify and to help develop special colors and designs, their ability must lie in dealing with finished products and combining them for the desired effect. The very diversity of the colors available to architects and interior designers in these finished products aids them in creating effective and artistically satisfying spaces. Until such time as the Universal Color Language truly becomes what it calls itself, with all color defined in a standardized manner, architects and interior designers must choose the systems most suited to their needs.

One simple and useful system is the chromatic circle, which uses red, yellow, and blue as its "primary" colors. While not in agreement with the physicists, it is very satisfactory for use by architects and interior designers. A large variety of colors can be obtained by mixing pigments of these three primaries, but as discussed later under the heading Paint, a knowledge of the qualities of the pigments themselves and of the way they mix is important. This aids in establishing the relationships of colors and the effects one has upon the other.

The chromatic circle (Plate 2) also shows what happens when the various colors are mixed together (i.e., red and yellow produce orange; yellow and blue produce green; and blue and red produce purple). On the chromatic circle, these are termed "Secondary Colors," and each is located halfway between two of the primary colors. "Tertiary colors," each situated halfway between a primary color and a secondary color, are obtained by mixing primary and secondary pigments (i.e., yellow and green produce yellow-green; blue and green produce blue-green, and so on around the circle).

The chromatic circle is a basic arrangement, each element of which can always be found in the same position. It provides simple color categories into which all pigment names can fall. In addition, it provides a tool which one can use in imagining the same colors with a change of value (brightness) and intensity in the three-dimensional manner such as that employed in the Munsell and Ostwald systems.

When an architect or interior designer is composing a color scheme for any given project, it is not as important to know the exact Munsell or Ostwald notation for a fabric color as it is to know that the fabric will be appropriate for its use, will look good in the type of light that is to be used, and will take its proper place with other colors that may subsequently be selected for paints, flooring, and furniture. In short, the architect or interior designer requires a simple system that permits the use of colors in appropriate relationships and that is flexible enough to use the many available products.

It should be recognized at the outset that good color schemes employ only a few colors, properly selected, mixed, and blended. The difference between good art and "calendar" art can be largely explained by this restraint. The professional interior designer uses many shades of just a few colors, while the amateur is inclined to use a great many more colors than are needed. By doing so, the amateur raises any number of problems and introduces so many conflicting notes that the result becomes unpleasant to behold.

The color schemes listed below are guideposts only, but guideposts which can be used with ease. After you have learned the rules, you can stretch and bend them, constantly analyzing the results of your variations and adding the findings to your store of professional skill and judgment. You may then not consciously think of the rules when you are designing in color, any more than a professional golfer thinks of the rules when playing in a tournament. The rules of color may be modified—or completely disregarded, as they sometimes are by the great painters. New color concepts may be formulated. But first, try the rules below; the results will surprise you.

One or two colors with black, white, or gray   This is the simplest of all schemes; the average book cover (without the dust jacket) is an example. Another would be an executive office having the walls covered with off-white grasscloth with a black pattern, two club chairs in medium-blue leather, and two side chairs in black fabric, with the carpet dark blue.

The monochromatic scheme   This scheme, simple but attractive, is one in which many shades of a single color are used. Of course, not all colors will lend themselves to a monochromatic scheme simply because the lighter colors cannot achieve deep enough values for emphasis. This limitation automatically eliminates yellow, orange, and pale green. A living room might be executed in a monochromatic scheme using walls of pale blue green with a wainscot of medium blue green. The carpet might be deep blue green. The sofa could be medium blue green, wing chairs in a deep blue green, and side chairs in a pale blue green.

The analogous scheme   The analogous color scheme permits the use of colors which adjoin each other on the chromatic circle (Plate 2), such as yellow, yellow green, and green, or red, red orange, and orange. These colors are not necessarily used in their pure form in various parts of the scheme, but are mixed together in varying amounts so that numerous shades may be developed from the few colors used. It is usual for one of the colors in such a scheme to predominate, that is, to be used in greater amounts than the rest. A bedroom might be developed as follows: Walls medium-deep yellow orange (copper); carpet pale gold (yellow); bedspread deep yellow orange (copper); wall hanging white, pale yellow, and medium orange; chairs pale yellow and white.

Analogous scheme plus complementary accent   A common type of color scheme consists of a series of analogous colors plus a complementary accent, i.e., a color on the opposite side of the chromatic circle from the center of the analogous run. For example, a scheme that uses yellow orange, orange, and yellow green could be combined with violet. By mixing these colors together in various amounts it will be found that the complementary accent (violet) will gray and soften the three analogous colors, deepen them for the darker tones, and at the same time complement them. This scheme might be used in a small cafeteria. The end wall could have a mural of a Japanese scene in black and white with yellow-orange accents. The sofas against the wall might be black; the chair seats might be yellow orange and white, orange and white, red orange and white, or turquoise and white (complementary accent).

Complementary scheme   For a simple complementary scheme, two colors opposite each other on the chromatic circle, such as blue violet and yellow orange, are used. Neither of these need be used in pure form; literally hundreds of shades may be obtained by blending them together in varying amounts. An interesting aspect of complements is the way the colors affect each other. In pure form they actually complement each other; each has the quality of making the other look better by its proximity. But as they are mixed together (as in paint or dye), they modify each other to the point where they finally form a neutral gray. It should be noted, however, that the neutral gray obtained by mixing different sets of complements will vary; sometimes a mousy gray occurs, and at other times a warm, brownish gray.

Grays can be formed in paint or dye by mixing any two complements, such as red and green, yellow and violet, orange and blue, or red orange and blue green. A tie score is as unsatisfactory in color as in a ball game, and since completely neutral grays seem to have no color at all, they are to be avoided or used sparingly. It is wise to use more of one complement than the other so that the resultant mixture clearly contains more of one color than the other. The same principle holds true in the selection of fabrics. Bright yellow, for instance, might answer your needs in a color scheme; but it is quite possible that a grayed yellow, made with a mixture of blue violet and yellow, would look better.

Another interesting phenomenon is that colors appearing in neither pigment sometimes appear when two complements are mixed. With certain proportions of yellow and blue violet, a rust color will appear. A little experimentation will illustrate this point. Using tempera, which mixes like most of today's interior house paints, mix the various complementary colors together in pans and watch what happens to each hue as it is blended in varying amounts with its complement.

A complementary scheme in a dining room might use blue green and red orange. One wall could be hung with a scenic wallpaper containing white, blue green, and some red orange, while the other three walls could be painted pale blue green. A carpet of taupe (a mixture of blue green, red orange and white) and curtains of red orange and blue green on white would complete the scheme.

Near, or split, complements   A split complement takes the form of a Y on the color wheel, the one arm of the Y pointing, for instance, to yellow orange, the other arm to yellow green, and the stem of the Y pointing to violet. A split-complement color scheme, then, is composed of a color plus one color from each side of the direct complement of the first color. This resembles the complementary scheme but provides a slightly wider range of colors and shades.

For example, red, yellow orange, and blue green might be employed in an executive's office as follows: Three walls would be papered in a pattern of blue-green and yellow-orange leaves and branches on a warm gray background, and the fourth wall would be covered with a blue-green grasscloth. The carpet would be beige, the executive's chair deep brown-red leather, and the side chairs medium blue-green leather.

Double split complements   A double split complement takes the form of an X on the chromatic circle with, for example, the top legs pointing to yellow orange and yellow green, and the bottom legs pointing to red violet and blue violet. These colors, used in a young girl's bedroom, might be distributed as follows: white walls, curtains of a print containing varied amounts of all four colors on a white ground, a bedspread of a yellow green, chairs with white frames covered in blue violet, and carpeting of a gray color obtained by mixing red, violet, and yellow green.

Triads   Another excellent color scheme may be obtained by the mixture of triads, that is, three colors located at the third points of the chromatic circle. For instance, red, yellow, and blue might be used in a traditional living room by having the walls and carpet off-white, the curtains a print of medium blue and pink on an off-white background, a sofa upholstered in damask containing grayed yellow and medium blue, and a wing chair and side chairs covered in a medium-blue fabric. The triad combination provides a wide range of hues, shades, and tints.

With all color schemes except the monochromatic, different kinds of colors and mixtures thereof may be obtained by varying the pigments that are used. In other words, the three different sets of orange and blue complements can be obtained by using three different kinds of blue on your palette, such as cobalt, french ultramarine, or cerulean. A red and green complementary color scheme permits the use of either Hooker's green or emerald green. A yellow violet complementary color scheme can be carried out with either cadmium yellow pale or yellow ochre.

Browns are a mixture of orange with blue, green, or gray; grays result from mixtures of three primary or two complementary colors. The type of gray—warm or cool—can be mixed to suit. It must be remembered that the colors represented in a scheme may or may not appear in the pure form. In a triadic color scheme, for instance, beige walls may be a mixture of yellow ochre, cobalt blue, alizarin crimson, and white. A wood color in the same room may contain the same colors, but in different proportions. A chair may be a shade of cobalt blue, a sofa of yellow ochre, a pillow of pure red, etc.

THE DEVELOPMENT OF THE COLOR PLAN

The creation of a color plan for any architectural space requires the application of established guidelines for creative reasoning, including:

1. Exploration of the field in which the problem arises.
2. Formation of a hypothesis (the solution of the color problem).
3. Development of the hypothesis to discover its implications.
4. Progressive testing and verification of the hypothesis by repeated observation.

1. Analysis

In solving a color problem, one would determine the following:

1. The proposed use of the space.
2. The size of the space.
3. The orientation of the space.
4. The type of people who are to occupy the space.
5. The length of time the space will be occupied by various people and their activities during that time.
6. The existing colors surrounding the space under consideration.
7. The client's (or clients') preferences regarding color and style. If these are incompatible with your findings, ways must be found to modify the client's thinking in order to preserve the integrity of the color plan.

When the analysis of the problem has been completed, certain decisions must be made.

2. Preliminary Findings

1. Determine the color plan that is to be used:
   a. One or two colors with black, white, or gray
   b. Monochromatic
   c. Analogous
   d. Analogous with complementary accent
   e. Complementary
   f. Split complement
   g. Double split complement
   h. Triad
   i. Other

The color plan must, of course, include the colors you desire for walls, floor, ceiling, furniture, and furnishings. For example, if you intend to use yellow on the walls, it is obvious that yellow must be part of the color scheme selected.

2. Determine the colors that will be used in each part of the room, and decide on their intensities. Color balance must be developed by carefully selecting areas and volumes that are to be light, dark, pale, or intense in color.

3. Evaluate the scheme for appropriateness.

4. Evaluate the colors in relation to each other to make sure that they are compatible.

5. Evaluate the colors and color scheme in the natural light of the space as well as the artificial light that will be used.

6. Make adjustments required by these findings and continue to refine and improve the color plan.

3. Development

The development of the color scheme will include the actual selection of materials:

1. Examine your collection of ready-mix paint colors to determine whether stock paints can be used. If the colors must be mixed on the job, it is well to experiment with these paint colors and tinting colors first so that you can intelligently direct the painter at the job.

2. Research the market for wood, wall coverings, furniture, fabrics, carpets, and other materials in the colors you require.

3. Evaluate your findings and modify, adjust, or change your color plan as necessary.

4. Experiment with variations of your final color plan to introduce individually.

4. Presentation to Client

1. When you are commissioned to work on a project, it is wise to ask your client to withhold all decisions or purchases with regard to color until you have had time to complete your study.

2. The presentation of a color plan to a client should be complete, clear, concise, and accurate. There should be no opportunity for misunderstandings.

3. Reevaluate all facets of the problem at this time. You can still change or modify items, if you so wish, before work is begun.

5. Execution of the Project

1. Be sure to communicate carefully and accurately with all persons involved in the ordering of all items. Order by company name, number, and color.

2. When deliveries of items are made, check again for accuracy.

chapter two

THE EFFECT
OF LIGHT ON COLOR

In the field of interior color, the expression "true color" has no meaning, because light is such a variable item. There are times when a room will be lighted by daylight only and times when electric or flame sources will be used. At other times both daylight and electric light will be present. By "true color," do we mean the color in daylight? If so, do we mean the color by daylight in the morning, at midday, or in the late afternoon? Do we mean true color on a hazy day or on a bright, sunny day? Do we mean the daylight of New York, Miami Beach, or Athens? All of these are quite different because of the differences in clarity of the air and other factors. A color probably becomes popular in one part of the world because it looks good in that particular location. In the past certain colors were widely used because they were pleasing in candlelight. The same colors look totally different under different kinds of electric light.

We know, then, that light modifies colors in an almost infinite number of ways. How can we apply this information to the use of color in interiors? First, we must realize that the colors we select or mix should be seen in the light in which they are to "live." The fabric on a chair may look good in a department store or showroom, but used in different light in the home, it may not be as attractive. A nubby fabric, well lighted, will have one color; in a dimmer light, it will have a duller color. Lighting arrangements must be carefully considered: Will colors be subject to spot lighting, reflected light, or diffused lighting? Will colored bulbs or colored filters be used? The skillful architect or interior designer will take all these factors into consideration when colors are being selected. Frequently adjustments will be made in the lighting or the color scheme as the job progresses.

Daylight

The colors that will be selected in, say, a house, will be determined in part by their location: Will they receive daylight from the north, east, south, or west? Generally speaking, one should use warm colors on the north, cool colors on the south, and neutral colors on the east and west. However, these colors are usually modified by other factors, such as the light reflected from other buildings and trees, the function of the room, and the prime hours of use of the room.

Incandescent Light

We must determine whether the electric lighting is to be incandescent or fluorescent, or a blend of the two. Incandescent light has a relatively large red component. There was a time when incandescent bulbs were the only type of electric light available, and they are still the most universally used type. Many people are accustomed to thinking of incandescent light as the norm, and since incandescent lamps are readily available in many different sizes, shapes, and intensities, they solve many lighting problems.

Inside-frosted incandescent lamps diffuse the light, eliminate striation, and help suffuse shadows. They are generally preferred over clear bulbs, but clear bulbs have many uses, as we shall see. Incandescent lamps (or bulbs) are generally used in portable lighting fixtures (popularly referred to as "lamps") or in fixtures which are hung from ceilings or attached to walls, most of which shade the bulb in one way or another. Such lighting fixtures can range from the most decorative to the most functional according to the requirements of the space in which they are to be used. Most of us are familiar with the 60-watt bulb, as well as the three-way combinations. These are but two of the wide variety of lamps which are available in many sizes and shapes—with up to 1000 watts of power for stage and studio lighting and other special situations. There are reflector-type bulbs and spotlight bulbs. Low-wattage reflector-type lamps can be used decoratively or functionally for specific lighting tasks. They are useful for pinpointing the light on a specific task or to accent special art work or displays.

Round lamps are available from 15 to 100 watts and range in size from 2 1/16 to 5 inches in diameter, both clear and in white. They are effective for display purposes or when used for a dramatic effect. Other imaginative incandescent lamps for decorative purposes are available in such shapes as flame and round and in finishes which are clear, frosted, beaded, or crystalline. Some are available in colors, such as blue, green, yellow, red, pink, silver, and gold.

Fluorescent light

When fluorescent light was first introduced, it was hoped that it would approximate daylight, but early results were disappointing. However, because fluorescent lighting is economical, great advances have been made to provide fluorescent lamps with a warm feeling similar to that of incandescent lighting. Available in today's market are such fluorescents as General Electric Company's Deluxe Warm White, which is very close to general-lighting incandescent—so close that many people would not be able to tell the difference in color rendition. Other fluorescent lamps are termed Warm White, Cool White, and Cool White Deluxe, although different manufacturers refer to them by their own trade names. Duro-Test has on the market a fluorescent which, the company believes, matches the visible and ultraviolet spectrum of natural outdoor light. It is the closest simulation of sunshine yet produced in a general-purpose fluorescent, according to their laboratory tests (see Figure 2.1).

Fluorescent lamps are offered in many different sizes and wattages, as well as a variety of lengths. All manner of fixtures are available, so that there are not only "proper" solutions for lighting problems but also esthetically pleasing solutions.

Fluorescents, while widely used in commercial, institutional, and industrial installations, are also popular for residential use. Often fluorescent light is combined with incandescent to create the proper atmosphere (see Plates 3, 4a, and 4b).

Fluorescent lamps designated warm emphasize yellow, orange, red, and red purple. The cool lamps emphasize blue purple, blue, blue green, and yellow green. The following is a guide to fluorescent lamp color:[1]

Warm White Deluxe:	Warm atmosphere, similar to incandescent Good color rendition Enhances warm colors Moderate light output
Cool White Deluxe:	Cool atmosphere—similar to midafternoon daylight Excellent color rendition Enhances all colors Moderate light output
C50:	Cooler atmosphere—simulates noon daylight Superior color rendition Enhances cool colors Cool blue-white Moderate light output
C75:	Coldest atmosphere—simulates north sky daylight Superior color rendition Enhances cool colors Cold blue-white Moderate light output

Here are some recommended uses of different-colored fluorescent lamps, from the same source:

Homes:
  Warm White Deluxe or Cool White Deluxe
Public Buildings:
  Museums .... Cool White Deluxe, Warm White Deluxe, C50
  Banks .... Cool White Deluxe
  Churches, hotels, motels .... Warm White Deluxe, Cool White Deluxe
  School cafeterias .... Warm White Deluxe, Cool White Deluxe
Offices:
  Reception areas, private offices, general
    offices .... Cool White Deluxe, Warm White Deluxe
Hospitals:
  Patient and reception rooms .... Warm White Deluxe, Cool White Deluxe
  Nurses' stations, corridors .... Cool White Deluxe

[1]General Electric Co., Lamp Business Division, Nela Park, Cleveland, OH 44412.

FIG. 2.1 Bathroom using Duro-Lite Vita-Lite
Duro-Test Corporation, North Bergen, NJ
Ernest Silva, photographer

Nurseries C50
Laboratories (color analysis) .... Cool White Deluxe, C50, C75
Treatment, examining, intensive care,
    operating rooms .... Cool White Deluxe, C50

Food Service:
    Restaurants, taverns .... Warm White Deluxe
    Cafeterias, bakeries, confectionery,
      delicatessens .... Warm White Deluxe, Cool White Deluxe

Retail Stores:
    Food, drug, clothing, variety .... Warm White Deluxe, Cool White Deluxe
    Women's wear, shoe stores, home
      furnishings, hairdressers .... Warm White Deluxe, Cool White Deluxe
    Jewelry, florists, hardware .... Cool White Deluxe, C50

Industry:
    Meat packing, inspection and display .... Cool White Deluxe, C50
    Dairy product processing, inspection and
      display .... Cool White Deluxe
    Baking and candy, inspection and display .... Warm White Deluxe
    Laboratories and paint manufacturing .... Cool White Deluxe, C50, C75
    Textile dyeing—color checking C50
    Printing and graphic arts
      Original art C50
      Press sheets C75

Structural Lighting

Structural lighting is usually fluorescent. It can be used behind curtain valances, wall brackets, cornices, coves, luminous wall panels, or diffusers; above luminous ceiling panels or floating canopies; under soffits; and in niches and coffers. It is not the purpose here to go into the design of these various installations, but a number of points are worth noting. In residential work especially, Warm White Deluxe is the perfect solution (see Plate 4b). The recesses of the several different types of installations should be painted flat white, and the lamps used in each element of built-in lighting should be from the same carton, since even a slight variation will be very obvious. All lamps should be of the same color and type, and both the channels and the lamp holders should be white. Remember that light which strikes a wall obliquely gives the wall a glowing quality. It is soft and uniform, but since the top of the furniture is lighted and reflects this light, one must be wary of cracked, rough walls. A rough plaster ceiling may appear to be soiled. Drapery materials used with such grazing light should have light backgrounds, and their patterns must be chosen with care. Designs of small figures are desirable, since the effect of the pattern will be accentuated.

The various kinds of built-in lighting are most effective when dimmers are used. These provide additional flexibility in the lighting design and mood.

When colors are being chosen (in a design office, for example) to be used under different light sources, it is wise to have examples of the different fluorescent lamps available so that the selection can be checked. A light box with four fluorescent tubes is very convenient, or a fluorescent-type desk lamp can be used and changed to suit each situation.

In Plate 3 (Kitchen), a flexible system provides the needed light. The counter tops are lighted by Deluxe Cool White fluorescent lamps (to enhance blue colors). The tubes are recessed into the perimeter of the ceiling, and a plastic lens shields them from view and directs the light down onto the counter tops. A pair of 50R20 lamps in downlight fixtures provides general illumination, and the decorative pewter fixture over the table identifies the dining area. Each system is switched individually.

Plate 4a illustrates the variety that can be obtained in lighting an executive office. The illumination of the desk by fluorescent lights is controlled to prevent glare but provide adequate light. Black ½-inch-cell louvers are used to shield the tubes. The draperies are highlighted by the use of PAR 38 lamps behind black louvers and refracting glass. Semirecessed filament units are directed at the wood-paneled wall and painting. A decorative table lamp using incandescent light is an effective addition.

Plate 4b shows the variation which can be provided in lighting in a living room. The table lamps and corner torchere are on three-way switches to provide flexibility. A 25-watt showcase reflector lamp and high-intensity lamp accent items on shelving. The fireplace wall is grazed by light from 5OR20 downlights on 32-inch centers. Warm White Deluxe fluorescent tubes behind the cornice wash the rear wall.

High Intensity Discharge Light

In their continuing search for more economical and better light, scientists are working on the improvement of existing lamps to increase their efficiency, overall performance, cost, and practicality. For instance, the Duro-Test Corporation has entered into a license agreement for exclusive rights to a new chemical film developed by M.I.T. Lincoln Laboratories. It is said that this film, when applied as an inside coating to a spherical light bulb, could reduce electrical energy consumption by 60 percent without any loss in light output.

While incandescents and fluorescents are the most widely used lamps, there is available a group of lamps designated High Intensity Discharge (H.I.D.), including mercury, General Electric's Lucalox, and the same company's Multi-Vapor. The early (1934) mercury lamp was relatively expensive, but its luminous efficacy was nearly twice that of incandescents, resulting in lower electric energy costs. It also provided a large quantity of light from a source small enough to permit easy maintenance and light control. The H.I.D. lamps offer excellent possibilities for the efficient use of electric energy. They are available in a wide variety of shapes and sizes, and their development and refinement for use in commercial and industrial interiors will no doubt continue. For example, in the case of the potential danger of ultraviolet radiation occurring when the outer globe of an H.I.D. lamp is broken, some manufacturers are solving the problem by equipping lamps with an automatic shut-off feature.

The following table indicates the characteristics of these lamps for interior general lighting, both commercial and industrial.

Deluxe White Mercury

Application: General lighting—store, commercial, and industrial
Optical controllability: Good
Glare control with typical fixture: Excellent

3. **Lighting design for kitchen**

General Electric Company, Nela Park, Cleveland, OH

(a)

(b)

4. (a) **Lighting design for executive office**
   (b) **Lighting design for living room**

General Electric Company, Nela Park, Cleveland, OH

Color effects: Accents—red orange, yellow, blue
                Grays—deep red, green

Warm Deluxe White Mercury

    Application: General lighting—store and commercial
    Optical controllability: Good
    Glare control with typical fixture: Excellent
    Color effects: Accents—red, orange, yellow, blue
                    Grays—green

Multi-Vapor Lamp

    Application: Industrial and commercial general lighting
    Optical controllability: Excellent
    Glare control with typical fixture: Good
    Color effects: Accents—orange, yellow, green, blue
                    Grays—deep red

Lucalox Lamp

    Application: Industrial general lighting; some commercial applications
    Optical controllability: Excellent
    Glare control with typical fixture: Good
    Color effects: Accents—orange, yellow, yellow-green
                    Grays—deep red, green, blue

Portable Lamps

Portable lamps enable one to adjust lighting to individual needs. The color and design of all the lamps in a room should relate to each other and to the furniture. Lampshades of certain colors—red in particular—should be used sparingly, since they tend to distort light. A colored shade is best lined with white, unless an unusual effect is required. Generally speaking, a lamp should provide for easy seeing. The primary light source is at the bottom of the lamp, but some light should come through the shade, and some should reflect from the ceiling. The height of the lamp should be adjusted according to the use: decorative, reading, working, and so on.

Reflectance

A surface, whether of paint or some other material, absorbs some light and reflects the rest. The amount of light that is reflected in proportion to the total amount falling on it equals the reflectance value of a color.

If one is designing the lighting for an existing installation, the amount of reflectance provided by the interior finishes must be taken into consideration when the required amount of light is being computed. In a new installation, the lumen method of lighting design requires that you know the reflectance of the colors of your interior finishes. A number of paint companies give the reflectances for each of their colors; you can judge the reflectance values of the colors you intend to use by comparing your colors with those whose reflectance values are known. Reflectance-value charts used by architects and designers are also helpful; in these, a number of shades of each color are shown, together with the reflectance of each. Reflectances of various kinds of wood are also sometimes indicated. The reflectance of any color chip or wood sample can be determined by comparing it with reflectances on a chart (see Plate 5). Needless to say, the colors that are used on any given job will be determined by reflectance value as well as other factors, such as suitability, individual taste, comfort, and the general aura or desired impression required of the job.

The quality of light in an area deserves great consideration in any situation. The use of the space will determine what qualities are required: A lobby or waiting area will use one set of guidelines, while an inner office requires another. However, within this framework there are usually three elements: walls, ceiling, and floor. A general guideline for reflectances is as follows:[2]

Ceilings: 60 to 90 percent (white or pale tint)*
Walls: 30 to 60 percent†

Window or glass wall (fabric treatment):
    Wide expanse or backgrounds .... 40 to 85 percent
    Limited areas of decorative design on light background or side
    draperies .... 15 to 45 percent

Floors: 15 to 35 percent (25 to 35 percent preferred)‡
    (Values at high end of range recommended for use in rooms where lighting efficiency is a major consideration—kitchens, bathrooms, utility rooms)

(In areas where lighting for special visual tasks takes precedence over lighting for environment, minimum reflectances should be 40 percent for walls, 25 percent for floors.)

* 70 percent or more is required for effective performance of indirect lighting methods.
† Appreciably higher than 50 percent creates brightness problems when portable luminaires are placed near walls and when extensive wall lighting methods are used. According to paint manufacturers, the public prefers 45 percent.
‡ Middle to high values preferred because of their predominance within the 60-degree cone of vision when performing many visual activities.

Munsell value scales for judging reflectances are also available. The reflectances of these scales were scientifically determined by direct measurement and by mathematical analysis.

In order to produce a visually harmonious effect, the reflectance values of the various elements of an area must be in balance. For instance, a bathroom with walls and floor of white tile and with white fixtures (items normally of high reflectance value) will appear more harmonious if carpeting and other accessories, including wallpaper or paint, are relatively dark in hue and of strong value to balance the reflectance. Similarly, in a bathroom where walls and cabinets, as well as tile, are darker in value and hue, luminescent panels can be used most effectively in the ceiling to provide balance for the low reflectance of the other components of the room (see Figure 2.1).

[2] Illuminating Engineering Society, *IES Lighting Handbook*, 5th ed., New York: 1972.

chapter three

THE PSYCHOLOGICAL
EFFECTS OF
COLOR

GENERAL

Various colors have a strongly emotional effect on people. It has been known for some time, for instance, that blue reduces excitability and therefore helps one to concentrate. Blue is both cooling and sedative, but it cannot be used indiscriminately, because too much of it may produce melancholia. These qualities of blue were discovered during the Middle Ages, and they are partially responsible for the use of so much blue in the stained-glass windows of the great Gothic cathedrals.

Green has a cooling quality and it acts as a sedative. Yellow, as one may note from sunlight, is cheery, stimulating, and attention-drawing. It is the most luminous color. On dull days, when the yellow of the sun is absent, most people exhibit mental and physical sluggishness and a general lack of enthusiasm for their work; when the sun appears again they become more active. Yellow also demands attention, and so it is used in dangerous locations, such as the edge of a subway platform, to mark the hazard.

Red is exciting and stimulates the brain. Medium red suggests health and vitality; bright red often has amorous connotations. Red also has an aggressive quality and is frequently associated with violence and excitement.

Purple, sedative and soothing, was orginally made from the Purpura shellfish of the Mediterranean. The dye from this shellfish, which was used for royal robes in ancient times, was so expensive that only the wealthy could afford it.

Orange has a stimulating effect and should usually be used in relatively small amounts. The occupant of an orange office, for instance, will become ill at ease after a short time and will leave it at every opportunity. Brown is restful and warming but should be combined with orange, yellow, or gold, because it can be depressing if used alone. Gray suggests cold and, like brown, is depressing unless combined with at least one livelier color. White, on the other hand, is cheerful, particularly when used with red, yellow, and orange.

Generally speaking, most people prefer either warm or cool colors. Personal preference depends on such factors as familiarity with various colors and color schemes and the emotional connotations, conscious or unconscious, that they have for an individual. A psychological reaction against the color blue, for example, may occur in a person who as a child was punished by being made to stay alone in a blue room. Similarly, a person will prefer colors that were present during pleasurable experiences. Thus, the color needs and desires of each individual must depend on a great many factors, the important point being that color likes or dislikes must be discovered before a color scheme is chosen. As Albers has said: ". . . we change, correct, or reverse our opinion about colors and this change of opinion may shift back and forth. Therefore, we try to recognize our preferences and aversions against what color dominates our work, what colors on the other hand are rejected, disliked, or of no appeal. Usually a special effort in using disliked colors ends with our falling in love with them."[1]

The great schools of painting have established characteristic color schemes, and those people who are fond of a particular period of painting will also usually be fond of the colors found in those paintings. The relatively low-keyed colors used by Rembrandt, for instance, are often found in the homes of those who are fond of Rembrandt's work. Similarly, the brilliant colors used by most contemporary artists are frequently present in the homes of those who admire contemporary art. The choice would seem to be a personal one.

There are, of course, other reasons for individual sensitivity to color. They will vary from the color-blind person to the person who is hypersensitive to color. Color sensitivity varies even among those with normal color vision. It sometimes changes with age and with the physical condition of the individual. A person who can usually tolerate a color may find it intolerable when he or she does not feel well. A person may like a certain color in small amounts, yet dislike a large area of it.

It ought to be clear, then, that color should be used with care. Designers may use whatever colors they prefer in their own homes, but they should not feel free to use any colors they like in public or commercial buildings. They must strive for a color scheme that will be attractive to a majority of the thousands of people who will use the building.

Since most people prefer a sense of order, they prefer a color harmony which is based upon an orderly plan. For example, a color scheme made up of colors that have something in common will appeal to most people. If the color scheme of a room is to be made of yellow ochre, cobalt blue, alizarin crimson, and white, the wall color may be made by mixing all three colors and

[1] Josef Albers, *Interaction of Color*, New Haven: Yale University Press, 1963, p. 25.

white, so that a beige results. The furniture, carpet, and color accents of the same room may be shades of the same yellow, red, and blue, or they may be made by mixing any of these three colors together in varying quantities to provide a "color family." Colors that are similar, such as yellow and yellow orange, or blue and blue green, will look good when used together since they are related.

Generally speaking, young children prefer brilliant bright colors, including the primaries, but as they mature their tastes may become more subtle. As time passes, a preference for more saturated colors again appears.

You may like a logically determined residential color scheme that you select this year; it may irritate you next year when you read in a popular magazine that the color scheme is no longer "in." On the other hand, the repainting of a famous old room will inevitably bring down wrath upon the head of the person who changes it if the new colors are not historically correct.

Demand for new products and ideas is created by changing people's tastes. Subjected to constant bombardment by the media regarding what is "new" and "desirable," the average consumer finds it impossible to resist the lure of the latest fad. However, restraint and common sense should be exercised before accepting every claim in the field of interior design. Mistakes in judgment can be costly, and most often an in-depth evaluation of the entire project produces satisfactory results. The work of such professional organizations as the Color Marketing Group is commendable, as they have done much to broaden the use of color in fashion and home furnishings for the average consumer and have provided coordinated colors among the many segments of the industry, such as paint, carpet, furniture, and fabrics, to supply variety and pleasing schemes for the average homemaker. Common sense, however, should tell one that what was truly beautiful last year will always be beautiful.

Although a great deal of color is selected emotionally, and even irrationally, guidelines do exist which, if used, help to keep the color designer on the proper path. The architectural space and all things in it must be studied as a unit to achieve an appropriate, as well as beautiful, color scheme. Color fixations must be dealt with, whether they are fixations of the designer or of the client. Certain shades of green and brown which are normally tolerated by most healthy persons may make someone who is not feeling well quite ill. A sufficient number of color changes normally exist in a residence to provide psychological contentment. But in large buildings it is often necessary to deliberately vary the colors in the different parts of the building so that most of the colors of the spectrum may be seen by the occupants during the workday. Color can be used functionally. We can make it draw attention to something—a wall, for example (see Plate 9)—or minimize its importance. We can make it maximize or minimize the size of objects. Color can be used to help express architectural forms—and, if carelessly used, it can destroy architectural form. Color on walls, floor, and ceiling is modified by other colors present in the same area. For instance, if three walls of a room are a warm gray and the fourth wall is a shade of yellow, the yellow will be reflected in the gray walls and will modify their appearance. Again, pale gray green may look good in a room until a bright shade of green is used next to it. Suddenly the gray green looks very gray and quite inadequate.

An enclosed room (i.e., one without an outside view) which is painted with warm colors makes those who work in it feel warm. Similarly, if a large, open, windowed space with a great deal of glass is painted with cool colors, people who work in it will sometimes feel chilly.

One is "prepared" for a room's color if the entrance is painted a complementary color. Deep colors always seem to make the walls of a room seem heavy, while pale pastel colors seem to make the walls light. If a room is long and narrow, its appearance can be modified by painting the end walls with warm colors—yellow, red, orange. Similarly, in a small room, the walls can be made to recede by painting them with cool colors, such as green and blue. A long corridor with many doors can be visually shortened by painting the two side walls different colors, the end walls in cool colors, and the doors each a different color.

From the above it will be seen that color can be made to modify form and, therefore, must be used with great care and skill if it is to help and not hurt architecture. An excellent amalgamation of color and architectural form may be seen in Plate 33.

As we mention in Chapter 5, color has been used in many different ways throughout history. Sometimes the palette has been quite limited, at other times diverse. The preference for color, even today, varies not only according to style but also by geographical location. Greenish blue with yellow and gray or white is popular in Scandinavian countries. In France, the traditional French colors are used in contemporary color schemes; these include, for example, the light green, light blue, and rose of the Louis XV period, the delicate tints of green, blue, gray, and dusty pink of Louis XVI, the rich, strong persimmon, orange, and yellow of the Directoire, and the deep green, yellow, gold, coral, and black of the Empire period. Even in the United States, which draws it taste from many lands, color usage varies according to location.

RESIDENTIAL

Colors used within the home must be tolerated by the whole family. If members of a family have tastes which differ widely, they may be satisfied by selecting the colors of their own rooms.

Residential color schemes, particularly those which are arrived at without any professional help, usually reflect current "taste" as seen in magazines or furniture stores. If these colors bear no relation to the location in which they are to be used, catastrophe frequently results, and a color designer is often called to correct the situation.

When a color scheme is being designed, certain problems arise immediately: Shall the walls be pale or deep in color? What parts of the room are to be light, medium, or dark in value (for contrast)? Shall the color scheme be cool, warm, or neutral? How sophisticated is the client? An interior space can be made beautiful in itself, but it will not necessarily complement the people who will use it. A skillful hand, however, can create a beautiful, restrained, and integrated colored space that will make its occupants look healthy and handsome.

A living room with a great deal of red in it will detract from the beauty of a woman's red dress. Couples should work together in selecting colors. The plan of living of a household group should be studied before any color selections are made. Someone engaged in a business which uses a great deal of energy should have a retreat at home—a room with a quietly harmonious color scheme. A person whose day is spent in a monotonous business, on the other hand, will probably enjoy color contrasts and bright colors at home.

As we have said before, most people prefer either warm or cool colors; this preference must be immediately determined. Next to be considered is the matter of personal color likes, dislikes—and fixations. The author has on a number of occasions worked with clients who would accept any color as long as it was shocking pink! Trying to dissuade such a client is like trying to take opium from an addict. Finally, the old stories about all shades of green being good for the eyes may have to be refuted, so that the client can be persuaded to use a certain suitable shade of green.

Approximately half of one's clients will like pastel shades and the other half deep colors. Sometimes those who prefer pastel colors have simply not had the courage to enjoy brilliant colors, and vice versa, or have not had the professional help they needed to choose well.

The architecture and orientation of a house or apartment will largely determine the colors that are to be used. A well-designed contemporary house may have colorful furnishings and accents. Walls or parts of walls are sometimes of natural-finished wood, stone, or marble. But architectural spaces which already exist do not always have such beautiful interior materials, and in these cases beauty must be obtained by applying paint, paper, etc., to walls and ceilings. Frequently an otherwise uninteresting dark space can be transformed by the use of sunny yellows, pinks, reds, tangerine, white or black, and warm lights. Bold colors stimulate conversation in a living room but should not be used in bedrooms, since their very brilliance may create insomnia. Often it is possible to bring deeper colors into such a space. The several shades of rust, blue, and yellow sometimes seen in stone outside one's room may be brought inside and used in a more brilliant fashion. While it is well to keep the major colors in a room low in key, walls, rugs, pictures, and furniture may be made brilliant with unusual colors such as lemon yellow, lime green, pink, and orange. The success of all colors used will, of course, depend upon their use in the specified location, the amount of each color, the light that will fall upon it, and the relationship of colors in each room to each other and to the central scheme.

COMMERCIAL

The commercial institution is a home away from home for many people, and the inclination to introduce some of the principles used in residential work is always present. But all the colors in such an installation must relate to each other and to a central scheme, and personal choice which conflicts with the appearance of the general scheme cannot be tolerated.

There are a number of reasons for such color control, the main one being that there is usually a certain amount of circulation of personnel; one sour note will stand out and become an object of ridicule. Members of a commercial organization must be willing to concede certain things for the good of all. Color likes and prejudices must not be permitted to enter the picture.

In most cases the walls of the lobby of a commercial building should be stimulating and exciting, and the corridors should be neutral, so that when the doors of the offices are open, harmony will be apparent. Individual offices may vary in color, texture, and materials, but they must have a basic similarity. The offices that will receive cold light, of course, should have warm colors, and vice versa; but within this framework certain small variations may exist. Even though orientation is taken into consideration in the selection of colors, each color must be tried during the design period in the exact location and in the kind of artificial light that will be used. If, in addition to general light, downlights and spotlights are to be used over pieces of sculpture, paintings, or other wall decorations, these should be switched on so that their effect can be noted.

While it is not the purpose of this book to suggest how works of art and accessories may be used in various offices, these items should be selected and positioned by the same person who designs the color schemes.

Although it is not possible to take into consideration the psychological needs of each worker in a large office, it is interesting to note that in cool-colored rooms some people will constantly complain about the cold or the air conditioning, while in rooms with warm colors some people will frequently complain that their air conditioning is not adequate. For this problem there seems to be no answer except to relocate the person.

Of course, the main objectives in determining the color scheme of a commercial installation are to provide colors which are rich, definite, and harmonious (see Plate 30), which will be easy to live with, and which will contribute to the efficiency and well-being of all who tenant the building. Colors should be subtle; for example, no brash greens or blues should be used unless compensating colors are used with them. Where offices are located upon an uninteresting interior court, the colors of such offices should be sunny and brilliant.

If all the above suggestions are followed, and if the color designer is allowed free rein, the installation will usually be psychologically satisfying. If, however, all the members of an organization are asked for their opinions, the results will be completely disastrous, since a successful color scheme cannot be designed by the consensus method.

INDUSTRIAL

As in the case of commercial installations, the kind of artificial light must be taken into consideration in the design of industrial interiors. It will depend, to a large extent, upon the type of operation performed. It goes without saying that a sufficient amount of light must be supplied. It is equally important that the proper *kind* of light be used to avoid shadows and glare. For ease of seeing, it is generally wise to keep the wall color darker than the machines or work benches. If the space under consideration is large, the walls should be in the cool category (blues or greens). If the space is small, the walls can be warm in color (yellow, orange, etc.). However, if intense heat is produced by some of the processes in a space, the walls should be painted a cool color, regardless of the size of the space, to psychologically assist the workers to bear the heat.

Similarly, in areas that are extremely cold, warm tones should be used on the walls.

Columns in nearly all industrial buildings should be brilliantly painted in yellow or vermilion to point them out to operators of trucks, forklifts, etc.

Safety Color Guides

The American National Standards Institute, Inc., in cooperation with the National Safety Council, has long promulgated a color code for marking physical hazards and identifying certain types of equipment in industrial plants. The use of color in this connection provides quick identification of danger spots even by persons who cannot read. Worldwide research is going on in other areas of safety such as highway marking, pictorial traffic signs that can be understood in all countries, and colors that can be identified by persons who are color-blind. Committees working on these projects encounter many problems, not only political and cultural but commercial, and decisions are sometimes slow to evolve. However slow, progress is being made to promote safety by the use of color and to reduce the number of accidents indoors and out.

Recently the United States Government passed the Occupational Safety Hazards Act, which covers many aspects of safety in places where workers are employed. The OSHA Safety Color Code (OSHA-ANSI Standards Z53.1, 1967) for marking physical hazards under this act designates specific colors for specific apparatus. Most paint manufacturers have colors in their lines which meet the Z53.1 standards. The standards are specified by both CIE and Munsell notations. However, they are constantly being revised; as soon as one set of colors is off the presses the revision process begins to achieve better results. It is wise, therefore, to keep abreast of new developments in this area.

The current OSHA Safety Color Code is as follows:

RED—Red shall be the basic color for the identification of (a) *Fire protection equipment and apparatus,* including blanket boxes, buckets or pails, fire exit signs, fire extinguishers, fire hose locations, fire hydrants, fire pumps, and fire sirens. In addition, post indicator valves for sprinkler systems and sprinkler piping should also be indicated in red. (b) *Danger*—Cans of flammable liquids; barricades or temporary obstructions; danger signs of all types. (c) *Stop*—Stop bars on hazardous machines; stop buttons or switches.

ORANGE—*Danger*
Dangerous parts of machines or energized equipment.

YELLOW—*Caution*
Marking physical hazards such as the possibility of stumbling, falling, tripping, striking against something, or being "caught in between." Solid yellow, yellow and black stripes, and yellow and black checkers (or yellow with suitable contrasting background) should be used interchangeably, employing the combination which will attract the most attention in the particular situation.

GREEN—*Safety*
First aid dispensary or kits, stretchers, safety deluge showers, etc.

BLUE—*Caution*
Caution against operation or use of equipment out of operation or being repaired.

PURPLE—*Radiation Hazards*
Purple can be used in combination with yellow for markers such as tags, labels, signs, and floor markers.

BLACK, WHITE, OR COMBINATIONS OF BLACK AND WHITE—*Traffic and Housekeeping*
This is the basic color combination for designation of traffic and housekeeping markings. Most recently, OSHA has approved the use of any clearly visible color to designate traffic and safety lanes. Many experts, however, prefer yellow to white, and OSHA has evaluated yellow as technically superior in most instances.

Piping Colors

In industrial plants and large buildings the piping is often complicated, and the following guidelines, from ANSI's "Scheme for the Identification of Piping Systems," are widely accepted:[2]

Color	Identification	Lettering
Red	Fire protection materials and equipment	White
Orange	Dangerous materials, nonflammable, such as acids, alkalis, toxic materials, gases, oxygen	Black
Green, Gray, Black or White	Safe materials such as drinking water, service water, brine	Black on Green or White White on Gray or Black
Blue	Protective materials	White

While in some cases piping might be painted an identifying color for its entire length (for decorative purposes, for instance), it is usually more successful to mark the pipe with an identifying band at one point and paint the rest the color of the wall or ceiling, which reduces visual clutter. One guide is to mark the pipe with a band where it enters or leaves the ceiling or wall, and perhaps again at periodic intervals. Banding at valves or joints is also desirable. The direction of liquid flow should be indicated. Banding should be done in the proper color, and the identification lettering should be visible at eye level.

Safety marking should be given adequate study for the best possible results. A fire extinguisher and hose mounted on a wall are clearly visible when a band of red is painted on the wall behind them. The section of wall or column occupied by the fire extinguisher and hose can be painted solid red from side to side and top to bottom of the apparatus. An additional band of red about 2½ inches wide painted on the floor beneath such protruding apparatus further identifies its location and helps warn passers-by of its existence.

Traffic lanes, trash containers, first aid equipment, stairways, columns in garages, etc., should be properly identified to avoid accidents.

INSTITUTIONAL

The interiors of institutions such as hospitals, youth detention centers, child care facilities, nursing homes, and mental health facilities are carefully studied in order to provide the most favorable environment for patients, visitors, and

[2] American National Standards Institute, Inc., 1430 Broadway, New York, NY 10018.

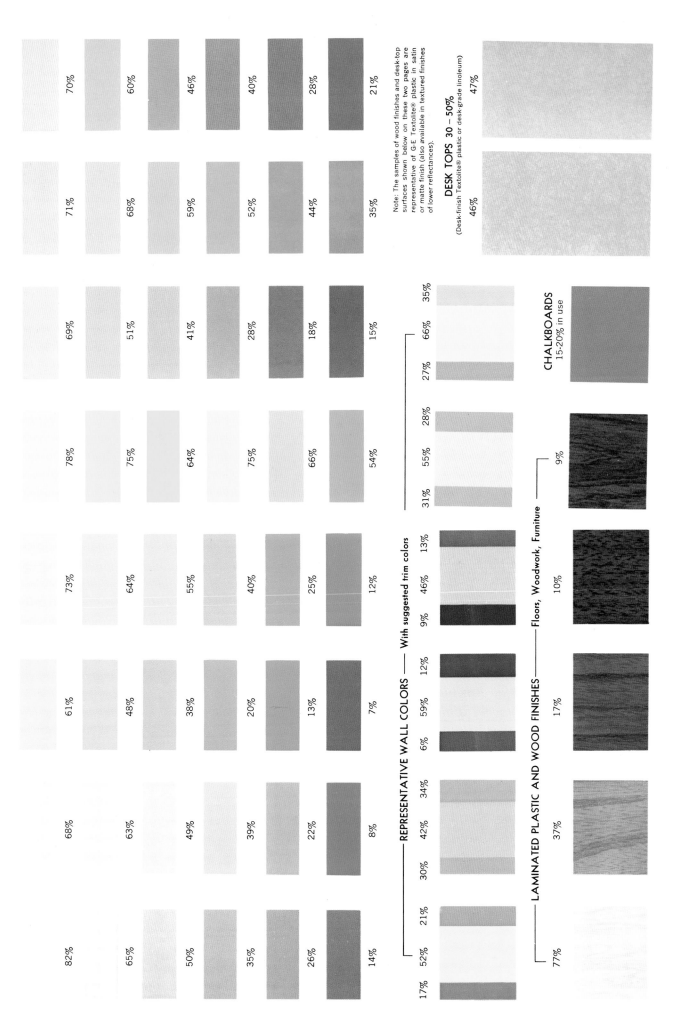

82%	68%	61%	73%	78%	69%	71%	70%
65%	63%	48%	64%	75%	51%	68%	60%
50%	49%	38%	55%	64%	41%	59%	46%
35%	39%	20%	40%	75%	28%	52%	40%
26%	22%	13%	25%	66%	18%	44%	28%
14%	8%	7%	12%	54%	15%	35%	21%

Note: The samples of wood finishes and desk-top surfaces shown below on these two pages are representative of G-E Textolite® plastic in satin or matte finish (also available in textured finishes of lower reflectances).

DESK TOPS 30 – 50%
(Desk-finish Textolite® plastic or desk-grade linoleum)

46% 47%

REPRESENTATIVE WALL COLORS — With suggested trim colors

| 17% | 21% | 30% | 34% | 6% | 59% | 12% | 9% | 46% | 13% | 31% | 55% | 28% | 27% | 66% | 35% |
| 52% | | 42% | | | | | | | | | | | | |

LAMINATED PLASTIC AND WOOD FINISHES —— Floors, Woodwork, Furniture

| 77% | 37% | 17% | 10% | 9% |

CHALKBOARDS
15-20% in use

5. Reflectance value chart

General Electric Company, Nela Park, Cleveland, OH

6. **St. Paul's School, St. Paul, Minnesota**
Lees Carpet of Antron II Nylon

Adkins-Jackels Associates, Architects, St. Paul, MN
David W. Hamilton, Photographer

staff. The aim should be to provide an atmosphere that is friendly and inviting.

Color and illumination are probably the most important of the visual elements. While pastel colors are most often employed in patient rooms, variety can be obtained by deepening the tone of the bed wall, painting the window wall plus an adjacent wall a deeper tone, or perhaps using a contrasting color on one or two of the other walls. If the room is an odd shape, the judicious use of two tones of color can help visually improve its proportions. A dado of wood or other material is an additional tool for providing color variation. The use of pattern to provide visual relief should be taken into consideration in the overall color scheme of patient rooms as well as other areas.

It has been observed that older patients appear to need saturated colors for easy identification, and this factor should be considered. In other studies it has been found that patients prefer different types of light color when examining their own appearance. For instance, blondes and brunettes have different preferences for illumination of their own skin color. As it is believed that patients' self-observations have a tremendous psychological influence on their well-being, it is advisable to provide more than one kind of illumination to answer different requirements.[3]

Reception areas, dining rooms, day rooms, libraries, and chapels can provide patients, staff, and visitors with welcome relief from the functional areas. Color, furnishings, and illumination can be varied to provide relaxing atmospheres. In Figure 3.1, showing the chapel in a county jail, the walls are a traditional soft, pale gray-green, with curtains of the same color. The pews and altar rail are stained brown mahogany with the end pieces painted off-white (actually a 4×1 letdown of the wall color). The altar curtain is scarlet, and red carpet covers the altar floor and aisle.

Figure 3.2 illustrates a hospital staff dining room for multifunction use. The walnut screens, columns, and chairs are complemented by a color scheme of yellow-orange, yellow, and yellow-green. The cornices are covered with a mottled-pattern vinyl in deep yellow-orange, and the vinyl for the pilasters is deep yellow-green. The abstract pattern of the curtains contains the three colors in lighter values on an off-white ground. The tweed carpet also combines the three colors and has black accents. Half of the chairs are covered in off-white vinyl and the other half in medium blue vinyl for accent. Variation in light control is achieved by opening or closing the curtains and by using a dimmer for the chandeliers.

Laboratories and specific examination areas such as X-ray, operating, and other treatment rooms may be attractively designed with cheerful colors. The use of wall graphics is often a good solution. There is no reason why an X-ray or radiology room cannot be treated in a decorative manner, despite the seriousness of the activity there. A quiet abstract graphic design on a wall, complementary to the color scheme, may provide just the right balance to the awesome equipment to remind both patient and professional that they are not isolated from the real world. The use of colorful utility cabinets and other accessories can also be considered.

In rooms with plaster ceilings, perhaps decorative ceiling lighting fixtures

---

[3] Dr. William Beck, reporting to Subcommittee 33, "Human Response to Color," Alexander F. Styne, Chairman; ISCC Newsletter, Annual Report Issue, No. 242, May-June 1976.

FIG 3.1   Chapel in County
Jail
Albert Halse,
A.S.I.D., Designer
Gil Amiaga,
Photographer

FIG. 3.2   Hospital staff
dining room for
multi-function use
Albert Halse,
A.S.I.D., Designer
Henry S. Fullerton
III, Photographer

can add the needed note of interest, or if the ceilings are high, they can be painted a color other than white. Vinyl wall coverings should also be considered.

As with any group of spaces, there should be a basic theme to unify the whole, but the individual areas should each reflect their own personality.

Long corridors can be used as a tool to unify; the lack of interest can be countered with art work and with colorful accents—unusual treatment of the ends of the corridors, of doors and frames, of periodical spaces, or of handrails, for example. The flooring in corridors should also receive careful attention, as it can be employed to good advantage to create areas of interest.

EDUCATIONAL

As mentioned earlier, although very young children prefer strong colors, when they grow older their taste becomes more sophisticated and subtle. In most contemporary schools almost anything that can be colored is treated in a bright and brilliant way. Corridor walls, for instance, are sometimes yellow; rooms facing cool north light are given warm tones, and those facing warm south light are given cool tones. The front wall of each classroom is often painted darker than the other walls of the room. Every effort should be made to select a color that will be of approximately the same value as the color of the chalkboard, so as to minimize eye fatigue. If colors are pastel, bright accents are employed for furniture and accessories—say bright blue, yellow, chinese red, or blue green. Doors and trim are usually darker than the walls in which they are located, and painted doors can be given variation and additional interest by the use of various colors.

However, while a stimulating atmosphere is desirable in a teaching situation (see Plate 6), care should be exercised to prevent overstimulation, which may produce restlessness, tension, and fatigue.

Establishments such as department stores and retail or specialty shops require special color treatments. Lack of space prevents us from including all this information here, but the reader will by careful observation be able to formulate guidelines similar to those given above. Each type of building has its own needs, and these must be analyzed before any color scheme is designed for a specific project.

chapter four

THE USE OF
COLOR FOR
IDENTIFICATION

Our various physical characteristics make us unique and serve to identify us from others. When we see familiar persons we can identify each one separately, perhaps by name, facial characteristics, speech, manner, or even profession. Countries, cities, and towns are also identified by unique characteristics. There are myriad ways in which we identify different objects or locations, and color is one of the easiest ways of making distinctions. But human beings continue to seek unique means of identification in preference to the obvious, more common ones. Some historians believe that the ancient paintings found on the walls of caves in France and Northern Spain were not only a means of decoration, but also served as a distinctive manner of identifying a particular tribe in the same way that American Indians used totem poles.

People have used flags and banners for identification since civilization began. After the discovery of weaving and dyeing in Egypt centuries ago, flags and banners were carried or displayed in numerous ways. At first simple streamers of cloth were attached to poles for use on ceremonial occasions. These were sometimes added to masks or other badges. Many early designs were religious; all were colorful.

In the Middle Ages in Europe, coats of arms of noblemen, designed by heralds, were extensively used. It was the duty of the heralds not only to announce their rulers' proclamations, but also to record the family history and rank and to prepare coats of arms and other emblems. Heraldry today is a sophisticated profession, engulfed in tradition and regulation, with terminology intricate and profound. The art is carefully controlled, not only as to the description of devices which may be incorporated in the design, but also as to the colors which may be used.

Coats of arms were used on shields and banners which identified units while traveling or while engaged in battle. Each country has a flag of its own which serves as a rallying point, whether in times of stress, jubilation, or celebration. Religious orders have long used shields and banners.

Local business and craftspeople, following the example of nobles and rulers, also adopted symbols which identified their specialty, such as the mortar and pestle of the chemist. English inns and taverns were identified by signs and symbols; the Old Red Lion Inn at Greenwich displayed a rampant red lion on a blue ground, while the "Sign of the Lion" at Barnert had a wrought-iron support which was cantilevered out into the road, so that the sign was extremely visible. At "The Chequers" in Steyning, Sussex, the banner of black and white checkered squares was also easily identifiable.[1]

At sea, too, flags were and are widely used as a means of identification and also for communication. At first a steamship company adopted a "house flag." Later this flag was painted on the masts of the ships, and then it was used as a trademark in advertising.[2]

The trademark was well established 2000 years ago.[3] Manufacturers and tradespeople have used such devices to distinguish their goods from those made and sold by others. The trademark served as a sign of integrity and quality. Ancient Roman terra-cotta and brick have been found showing not only the manufacturer's or owner's name, but also the factory where it was produced and, occasionally, the estate where the clay was found, as well as the name of the consul, the emperor, or the member of the imperial family for whom the building was constructed. Medieval stonemasons developed complicated marks, which were variations of the cross, to identify their work. With the development of book printing came the printer's colophon and mark. Early signs were based on variations of the orb and cross. In Oriental countries family crests are a tradition.

Trademarks have been copyrighted in the United States since 1877, when the Smith Brothers (of cough-drop fame) produced their now famous simple concept of the heads of two bearded gentlemen in black and white. To be effective, a trademark should be composed of simple elements—circles, squares, and triangles—and it should be easily recognized and colorful. Symmetry establishes equilibrium.

Trademarks are an important factor in our competitive world in creating an "image" of a business corporation for the public. Most of us can identify many such trademarks, hundreds of which are known internationally. Carrying this symbolism further, it can be used in dozens of ways on an organization's products or on an institution's stationery, tableware, and other items. It follows very logically that architects and interior designers should look to these symbols to inspire interior designs, wall decorations, and art work. As well as identifying

[1] H. Donaldson Eberlein and A. E. Richardson, *The English Inn Past and Present,* Benjamin Blom, Inc., Pubs., 1925.

[2] Gordon Campbell and I. O. Evans, *The Book of Flags,* London: Oxford University Press, 1969.

[3] Egbert Jacobson, *Trademark Design,* Chicago: Paul Theobald & Co., 1952, p. 1.

particular areas, they help to direct visitors wherever they are going and, when they have arrived, to reassure them that they are in the correct place. Many worldwide organizations deliberately employ certain special means—whether color, layout, or furnishings—in all their establishments to give the traveler a sense of security and familiarity even if in a strange locale.

This method of inspiration can also be adapted to residences. Unlimited original designs and colors can be used in homes or special rooms to make them truly unique. Some places are identified with great works of art; in others, symbols and abstract designs are used on walls (see Plate 7, Kitchen Renovation), or in wall hangings in the form of tapestry, carpet, or embroidery. The designs of fabrics can take their inspiration from the same source and colors from these designs enable the whole room or building to establish a unique identity.

COMMERCIAL

In an airport installation, Braniff International[4] integrated its identifying initials "BI" with nonrepresentational carousel designs and used variations of these designs in different areas of the facility. A ceramic wall is designed with the letters BI (see Figure 4.1), and a custom-designed vinyl wall covering repeats the design and colors in another area. The trademark is etched in glass doors and partitions. The carousel design is used in corridors and on banners with varied color schemes. The yellow-gold background color of one corridor has one wall decorated with the carousel pattern in vivid hues of magenta, red, orange, green, purple, and blue. Banners hung from the rather high ceilings in other areas repeat the carousel pattern with predominantly green, purple, or blue color schemes (Plates 8a and 8b).

In a showroom, the visitor is greeted by a carpeted area with a giant graphics pattern in navy blue and red to point the direction to where the sign of the company is prominently displayed in three-dimensional white letters (Plate 9). Such primary colors as navy blue and red are used for startling effect, while the company's display is surrounded by white for a dramatic contrast. There is no question of identification.

Another commercial enterprise displays its trademark with a three-dimensional sign in red on a dark blue wall. In front of the wall is a white desk, providing the receptionist with an elegant setting for her role.

Department stores and other retail establishments constantly face the competitiveness of the marketplace, and they employ color, combined with graphics, to identify themselves and their individual departments, such as the boutiques of famous designers or other areas with specialty merchandise.

INSTITUTIONAL

In an elementary school, a carpeted pit is often the focal point for reading or discussion sessions. When the walls are treated with a free-flowing, colorful abstract pattern, the flowing lines of the pit are echoed (Plate 6). The bright orange, gold, blue, and greens of the wall pattern are in direct contrast to the medium blue carpet.

[4] *Interior Design*, "Braniff International Terminal, Dallas/Fort Worth Airport," November 1974.

FIG. 4.1 *Braniff International, Dallas/Fort Worth Airport*
Harper & George, Designer, New York, NY

In another reading pit, facing upon one end of the classroom, the uncovered structural steel beam and columns are painted a bright orange in contrast with the neutral dark tones of a wood partition. The letters of the alphabet in white, both capital and small letters, are used to decorate the lower edge of the partition, combining both the decorative and the informative to the advantage of the students. In this school, such forms as a cutout paper doll are used to decorate a bright blue wall, and a large arrow points in the direction of the toilets (Plate 34).[5]

In another preschool open classroom, primary colors and basic forms are used to decorate walls. One wall has a large horizontal band of orange which

[5] Mount Healthy School, Columbus, Indiana; see *Architectural Record*, September 1973.

leads one's eye to the door. The door itself is enlarged to a yellow and blue triangle, with the actual door standing out in red.

Medical environments offer a great challenge to architects and interior designers, not only with regard to furnishings, but also with regard to color for the various areas. Such projects deserve a great deal of research and study aimed at producing a better understanding of the relationship between color and how humans respond to it. A sterile-looking room will do little to encourage the patient's recovery, and ways are being found to make the hospital environment more reassuring without infringing too deeply on the budget. Interesting innovations are being carried out in other specialized areas; for example, in a pediatric area a carpeted play pit with variations in levels may be provided to keep young patients comfortable during their wait. Wall decorations could consist of happy clowns in cheerful colors to engage the youngsters' imagination. A dental care unit might be decorated with comic-book characters—including the famed "Snoopy"—all taking care of their teeth or showing off bright smiles. Surely such an environment helps alleviate to some extent the fear and anxiety that some children experience when visiting these facilities.

A dramatic treatment of elevator doors and cabs can be an important element of any interior design. At the Monroe C. Gutman Library at Harvard University, the elevator doors are a bright spring green, which is extremely visible in the exposed concrete walls. The interiors of the cabs are treated as works of art; one has a sphere of bright orange in a field of yellow, while a companion cab contains a sphere of yellow in a field of orange (see Plate 33). The color of the carpeting is carried through the department, and the furniture in neutral wood tones is complemented by appropriate upholstery.

SOURCES OF INSPIRATION

Interior designers and architects are fortunate in having a variety of sources from which to obtain elements to carry out a scheme—for example, simple wallpaper patterns, special symbols, or original artists' designs that can be applied to a wall area. Winfield Design Associates of New York and the Artafax Systems available through Robert Benjamin in New York are two examples. Using acrylic paints, one can obtain a variety of designs in special sizes and colors, all carefully executed on fine paper which is then stretched and framed in one of several ways. Acrylic plastic (¼ inch thick) with a plastic frame may be used, or aluminum sheets in sizes up to 48 by 54⅔ inches. Photo-graphics provide another variation of this type of decoration.

Yet another solution is offered in a series of nonrepresentational designs, some in multiunit paintings which, when installed, make an oversized display. Executed on mounted canvas, or protected inside acrylic sheets, these are excellent solutions in areas of high traffic where maintenance is a problem. Flexibility and versatility are the advantages of this system.

Another approach to the provision of wall decoration is the use of functional graphics, such as arrows pointing the way, male and female silhouettes for rest rooms, or question marks for information areas. They, too, can be produced on stretched artist canvas or acrylic or aluminum sheeting in colors of your choice.

The use of original paintings, tapestries, or other works of art is indeed effective if the environment is suitable and the items are unlikely to suffer any harm. Similarly, designs applied directly to walls are often the proper solution, but great care must be taken in the preparation of the wall, and the craftsman or artist should be skilled in this type of work to produce a satisfactory result. The question of maintenance should be considered when designs are applied directly to walls.

chapter five

FACTORS CONTRIBUTING TO CONTEMPORARY COLOR USAGE

This book is devoted to a study of the contemporary use of color in the fields of architecture and interior design. We shall look briefly at the historical use of color, since this will help us understand why we use color as we do today. We can thoroughly appreciate the use of color in other periods only if we know the general history of those periods. Many books are available for this purpose. We should study the manner in which the scientist and painter look at color, but we must never confuse these approaches with the arts of architecture and interior design: They are simply not the same. The skills and knowledge of the painter and other artists do not alone make them capable of using color in architecture or interior design any more than such skills make them architects; nor does the cold analysis of the scientist make him or her an expert in interior design. Each contributes and inspires, but the architect or interior designer alone devotes a lifetime to the application of color in genuine architectural situations.

People in all periods of history have contributed some knowledge to the use of color in architecture and interior design, and there have been rich periods and barren ones—periods when a great deal of color was used and periods that might be termed drab. Although it is not our intention to explore this history at length, a brief look at the most important historical periods is important to the understanding of today's use of color in in architecture and interior design.

EARLY PERIODS

Prehistoric

People in prehistoric times probably spent all their time and energy in the struggle for survival. But even when they killed or were themselves in danger of being killed, the desire or need to express themselves by drawing and painting was strong enough to cause them to record in the feeble light of their caves those animals and objects that they saw during their daily existence. Some paintings may also have been made in their less permanent structures, but this we do not know. Using red and yellow ochre for drawing, and the same earth colors ground into a powder and mixed with animal fat for painting, ancient artists produced pictures of bison, reindeer, wild boars, mammoths, and other animals, such as those on the walls of the cave at Altamira in Spain (15,000 B.C.) and at Font-de-Gaume in France (15,000 B.C.).

No one knows, of course, whether these drawings were for the purpose of guarding ancient tribes against evil or guaranteeing good hunting, but the author likes to feel that they were an attempt by human beings to brighten up a primitive living space and make it something special and precious that they could retire to after the rigors of their almost impossible existence.

By the Mesolithic and Neolithic periods (20,000 to 2000 B.C.), people began to domesticate animals, to grow grain, and to live in permanent homes. Writing, indicated in the painted pebbles of the Azilians, began about 10,000 B.C. A few pieces of textiles, together with bundles of fibers, loom weights, and spinning whorls, have survived from this period.

Egypt

The materials at hand, the climate, and the richness of a civilization have always guided its artisans. In the realm of the pharaohs the sun was brilliant and the climate warm. Natural products such as timber, stone, and clay were available. Among the stones found most useful by the Egyptians were limestone, sandstone, syenite, and red granite.

In the Valley Temple of Kahfre (2850 B.C.) the supports and lintels were of red granite, well-proportioned, and cut and polished with proficiency. The floor was finished with slabs of alabaster. Columns in many other stone temples were richly decorated in color, and both exterior and interior walls were carved and painted. The ceilings of some temples were blue, probably to represent the sky, and the floors were often green, like the surrounding fields. Some authorities believe that color and decoration in ancient Egypt may have been symbolic; for example, Osiris was usually represented by green, his wife Isis by blue, and their son Horus by white.

The paint, a kind of tempera, was apparently applied in flat tones with no blending or shading. While we can only surmise the many colors that were available to the Egyptian artist, we can see in the Metropolitan Museum of Art in New York City a fifteenth-century-B.C. palette which contains medium and yellow ochre, terra-cotta red, turquoise blue, green, white, and black. These paints were no doubt made from burnt bones for black; malachite for green; oxide of iron for pink and red; red and yellow ochre; cobalt for blue; crystalline compounds of calcium, silica, and copper; and arsenic trisulfide, which made a bright lemon yellow.

Most murals were planned as storytelling devices which recorded daily life and religious functions. A frieze painted on plaster in the Tomb of Atet at Meidum (2725 B.C.) has two handsomely drawn geese painted in black, gray, white, and red on a grayed background. The realistic foliage is rendered in a yellowish green. A painted limestone relief dated 2550 B.C. includes golden yellow, black, gray, and orange. Later paintings included golden yellow, black, an orange red, and brilliant yellowish green.

A painted limestone relief from Abydos (1991–1785 B.C.) shows the first use of cobalt blue with red figures in a geometric pattern. Cobalt blue, red, golden yellow, and black were used in a wall painting depicting birds being hunted with a throw stick (1400 B.C.).

Sculpture in the round included bowls, vases, heads of birds, and male and female figures. Many of these were finely painted. The sculptor of a statue of a princess (2900–2750 B.C.) used rock crystal for eyes, yellow for the skin, red for the lips, black for the hair and eyebrows, and red and blue for the necklace. A small figure of painted clay (237 B.C.) shows a painted green "skirt," and a clay vessel has a reddish-brown painted design.

Examples of wood furniture, used by royalty and the well-to-do, have been found, including chairs, chests, beds, and tables. Many are carved and painted, and such motifs as palm, lotus, papyrus, lion, cobra, and ibex were used as decoration. Although little is known of the colors used for Egyptian furniture, ivory and ebony were used as inlay, and gold ornament was applied to woodwork. The back support of the King's throne from the tomb of King Tutankhamen and his Queen uses gilded wood with inlay of silver, faïence, and colored blue and green enamel (1340 B.C.). During the same period, dark blue was sometimes used against a lighter blue background.

The colors used in ancient Egypt varied greatly from those of the prehistoric era (fifth to third millennia B.C.) and from those of the Ptolemaic and Roman periods (approximately 304–30 B.C.). In the Old Kingdom, painting was applied on reliefs; in the Middle Kingdom, the painters sometimes eliminated reliefs and painted directly on the walls or on stucco or plaster applied to rough walls. These wall paintings, a part of the Egyptian funerary art, were similar to those of the ancient periods. The later periods, dominated by aliens, show the use of traditional black, red, and white on light backgrounds, iridescent blue-purple-green faïence vessels, and bronze statues. Gradually, however, Greek and Roman elements appear in more definite form until even the god Horus is shown dressed as a Roman legionary.

The cultures of Egypt, Babylon, and Crete existed simultaneously for thousands of years. A similarity in the arts of these peoples indicates some interchange of ideas. The Babylonians used baked brick, glazed tiles, and friezes. On the island of Crete, the Palace of Knossos (3000–1500 B.C.) had foundations of stone blocks and columns of wood with block bases, all brightly painted. There were wall frescoes depicting Cretan life, and there were colored plaster ceilings. Mural paintings included scenes of bullfights and ceremonies, and many scenes included pictures of fish, flowers, birds, and animals.

Greece

The Greeks, a colonizing and trading people who had contacts with the peoples of Egypt, Phoenicia, Babylonia, and Assyria, were inspired by the use of color in those lands. The climate of Greece, more diversified than that of Egypt, was semitropical, and there were variations in temperature and in the amount of moisture. The land was beautiful and inspirational. The homes of the early Greeks seem to have been unpretentious, and it could almost be said that they were more interested in life than they were in their physical surrroundings. Religion played an important part in the lives of the Greeks and they carved statues of their gods and built temples to protect these statues. During the early periods the temples were of wood, but by 600 B.C. temples of stone began to appear. The proportions and details of these stone temples became more and more refined. The highest development of Grecian art occurred in the construction of a group of religious buildings, among them the Parthenon, on a hill called the Acropolis (447 B.C.). Marble, which took a high polish, soft white stone, and limestone were used for exteriors and interiors of these temples. All features of Greek architecture were functional. Structural surfaces were adorned only when such adornment emphasized, rather than hid, the structure. Color was used to accent the unity of design. Stone buildings such as those on the Acropolis were usually painted, the color being concentrated in the upper portions of the buildings. Blue and red were used in greatest amounts, but black, green, yellow, and gold were also used. Triglyphs were blue; metopes and stringcourses, as well as parts of the cornice, were red. Thus it may be seen that color was used to emphasize the various parts of the building.

A great deal of architectural decoration, both in relief and in the round, was painted in the conventional (not naturalistic) manner. Subject matter for sculpture was liberally taken from plant and animal life. Many of the motifs, such as the acanthus leaf and the lotus bud and flower, are still used today. Geometric patterns were also widely used and include nonrepresentational fret and mosaic patterns, all of which were brightly colored. The human figure was used for decoration and for both marble and bronze sculpture. Although there are few remaining examples, the statuary of the ancient Greeks was brightly colored, the marble figures being painted yellow, red, blue, and green. Sometimes stones of great value were used to represent eyes.

Because of the great need for containers for liquids such as honey and oil, pottery making became an important art, and, interestingly enough, much of the day-by-day life of Greece was used as subject matter in decorating this pottery. Occasionally geometric patterns were used, but many times a story is told with human and animal figures. Early pottery was purple and white; later it was glazed in black on reddish clay. The later pieces show figures and patterns of red on a black background. Refinements were constantly being made, and in the sixth and fifth centuries B.C., for instance, vases were produced which used the black on terra-cotta; panels not covered by black were painted with black figures.

Over the centuries, the Greeks developed a keen sense of refined beauty in which all the elements of a building were studied for balance, proportion, and harmony. Sculpture, carvings, and color were employed to heighten this refinement. Although Greece began to lose its political importance after the death of Alexander in 323 B.C., its architectural influence continued in other lands.

Rome

Although the civilizations of Greece and Italy developed about the same time, that of Greece developed more quickly, coming to its greatest height in the fifth and fourth centuries B.C. The Etruscans, culturally similar to the Greeks, probably emigrated from Asia Minor and were in control of most of Italy. They lived in heavily fortified cities, and their homes were brightly decorated. However, the best of the Etruscan paintings that have come down to us were painted on the walls of chamber tombs. Unfortunately many of these were destroyed by atmospheric conditions once the tombs were opened. The subject matter of the tomb paintings included gay, lifelike scenes of banquets, sports, music, and so on. These tombs, which only the wealthy could afford, were connected to the home of the family. Painting was not very often used on anything but walls, stone sarcophagi, and terra-cotta urns.

Of the wall paintings, the most important are from the Necropolis of Tarquinia. Here we find a series of paintings which date from the middle of the sixth century B.C. The subject matter is, for the most part, taken from Greek mythology, and human figures are painted in a shade of red upon a lightly colored background, horses in an off-white and red, trees brown, and leaves green, all in a very stylized fashion. Gradually the Greek influence waned, and Greek forms were recast and varied so that they became representative of the strength of the Roman Empire. Subjects included warriors, horses, flags, shields, etc., all contained between borders of ornament. Off-white backgrounds were sometimes used. Colors included black, brown, red, and a golden yellow.

Some large figure compositions showing gods and goddesses·are painted with deep blue backgrounds and white, pinkish-red, and green clothing. They show a great deal of detail. Some paintings use warm flesh tones together with red and black, while others use flesh and warm tones for figures and clothing and green or white for the background. Still-life paintings also include the use of this complementary color scheme. Other still-life paintings use birds, snakes, and flowers painted in bright colors on dark, almost black, backgrounds.

Mosaics seem to have followed the same color pattern as the wall paintings, with flesh tones set against black and white and with the occasional use of a blue green. As time passed, the paintings and mosaics became more complicated in composition and more delicate in color.

The invading armies of Rome brought back with them many Greek works of art and many Greek artists. The Romans, masters of the more practical arts of building, seem to have been satisfied with the use of imported artists and imported works of art for the decoration of their great public buildings. Most of the color and texture of the public buildings, however, was obtained by the use of the materials themselves: marble, alabaster, porphyry, and jasper for walls, and marbles and mosaics for floors. There were also mural decorations in fresco.

What little we know about the paintings of these times we have learned through a study of the works in Pompeii. Many were in small or private buildings that were preserved for centuries by the lava of Vesuvius which destroyed that city in A.D. 79. A great many decorative mural paintings were made between the second century B.C. and A.D. 80, and from this period we have numerous examples of Pompeian paintings. Walls were painted to imitate marble facing; friezes were painted; the artists seem to have struggled to cover the walls with architectural fantasies, perspectives, "outside" windows, and doors. Later painting seems to have used architectural scenes less often, and the walls were divided into many colored panels with carefully painted linear patterns containing human figures and animals. Backgrounds were yellow, red, green, and black. Information gathered during the excavations seems to indicate that the colors available to the artists of that period included a white made from pumice stone, a green earth pigment, blue, scarlet (pink), brown-red ochre, and a yellow ochre.

By A.D. 300, Rome, although visually still magnificent, had become decadent, and its influence was soon to wane.

THE MEDIEVAL PERIOD

Constantine, by moving his capital to Byzantium (which he renamed Constantinople) in A.D. 330, divided the Roman Empire into two sections, East and West. Christianity, spreading from the eastern Mediterranean through Constantinople to Rome, produced many outstanding church buildings that varied in style according to location. In such lands as Persia, Egypt, Asia Minor, and Syria, Christian buildings followed somewhat the architectural traditions of these older civilizations, while in Rome they were influenced by existing Roman architecture. It was at powerful Constantinople, with its strategic location, that Roman and Eastern influences merged to become what we now term the Byzantine style. Western Europe, invaded by barbarians, now found itself amid the remains of the Roman imperial culture mixed with the primitive ideas of the invading hordes. Church building gradually ceased, lacking the strength and direct influence which the builders of churches in Rome had supplied. In the East and in Constantinople in particular, art and architecture began to be modified by such factors as the dislike of the early Christian for anything pagan, the Semitic dislike for the representation of sacred personages, and the influence of Islam, which set the stage for an image-destroying attitude that resulted in the use of architectural ornamentation employing geometric and floral motifs, the use of texture, and rich color. No single age has left us so many large, liberally decorated monuments—the decoration varying, of course, with location. Because of the development of mathematics in Egypt, areas in contact with that country show a great deal of geometric ornament. In Rome pictorial treatment of wall and door surfaces continued, as in earlier Italian architecture. The Romanesque church used polychromy for sculpture and also used mural painting. The Middle Ages, well known as a period of great stone sculpture, were also a great age of painting, especially great story-telling paintings. Textiles were used as well. In this period, walls, vaults, and the intrados of arches were frequently painted in manner reminiscent of the ornamental bands of manuscript decoration.

Color was often rich in some parts of what is now France, and such colors as violet were used. In other parts of the same area, colors were lighter in tone and included red ochre, yellow ochre, black, white, and cinnabar. Green was rarely used, and blue was usually reserved for representations of the garments of Christ.

Recently the altarpiece in the Church of Ambierle, 60 miles northwest of Lyons, was restored. This Gothic church, dating from the end of the fifteenth century, contains beautiful examples of stained-glass windows, but the treasure is the altarpiece, 7 feet high and 9 feet long when closed and twice as long when open. Its sculptured fixed portion tells the story of the Crucifixion, while the movable panels are covered with portraits of the family of the donor and their patron saints. The carved figures are of walnut, available in the south central portion of France, and the case is of oak, used mainly in the north. It has not been definitely established whether this altarpiece is a Flemish or a Burgundian work of art.

The restoration of this altarpiece was undertaken by France's Direction des Monuments Historiques. Broken pieces of the sculpture were meticulously restored, and delicate borings were made to find the original colors. Wherever colors were lacking, the artists proceeded by deduction and constantly referred to other similar works of that period. The carved figures of the main portion are in various shades of red, white, occasionally blue green, and brown, against the gilded tracery background. The painted panels show figures in costumes of red, yellow, and black, while the trompe-l'oeil statues on the outside are white in niches of crimson.

In Italy, the early painted pictures on wooden panels expressed the beauty of the Umbrian, Tuscan, and Sienese landscapes; they were often on parts of a chest, altar, or door. These brightly colored paintings were the forerunners of modern painting. During the last part of the fourteenth century and the beginning of the fifteenth century, the brilliantly colored miniature landscapes depicted houses in pale yellow, coral, pink, and white, usually on backgrounds of dark olive-green hills.

Many examples of the art of this period can be seen in the famous collection at The Cloisters of New York's Metropolitan Museum of Art. The six tapestries representing "The Hunt of the Unicorn" are worthy of note because of the harmony in the use of the colors. The reds, yellows, blues, and orange are used dramatically to emphasize the white unicorn, and the green and blue-green foliage provides a subtle background to enhance the many details. Unfortunately it has not been possible to establish without doubt whether these renowned works of art are of Flemish or French origin.

Other monuments to this great period in history include the Cathedral of Notre Dame at Chartres, started in 1150, Notre Dame in Paris, started in 1163, the Cathedral at Rouen, 1200, and Rheims, 1211. In England, Salisbury Cathedral was constructed between 1220 and 1258, and Westminster Abbey was begun in 1250. Much time, effort, and money was expended in the beautification, including the coloring, of these religious structures.

THE RENAISSANCE

The Italian Renaissance

The Church, with its center in Rome, had become extremely powerful during the medieval period, but with power came a decay in morality. This, combined with heavy taxation, set the stage for a reaction against the suppression of human emotion and thought. Color returned to buildings used by the living and was employed to express the enjoyment of life and nature. The Church, powerless to suppress further the interest in the works of antiquity, took them for its own, and with them, classic color.

The wealthy merchants of Italy became patrons of the arts, and they built and decorated enormous palaces. These were decorated with painted frescoes, embroideries, and tapestries. The scenes used in the murals included antique ruins, religious and classic subjects, and often important happenings in the history of the patron's family. Often the colors in the murals determined the other room colors and the colors of accessories. Between 1400 and 1500, marble slabs were used in wall treatments and for trim, the field often being of one color, the moldings another. Gold was sometimes used on the capitals of columns and pilasters, as well as on ornamental cast-plaster objects.

During the early part of the Renaissance, less wealthy merchants built smaller country villas. In these, expensive architectural forms were usually omitted, and richness was obtained inexpensively by painting imitation textiles, complete with folds, on sand-finished plaster walls. Wood-beamed ceilings were vividly striped with paint, and wood-paneled ceilings were often covered with arabesques, scenes, or ornament. Floors were often made with terrazzo and with colored or black-and-white marble and tile. Wherever economically feasible, the color of natural materials was used. Imitation painted "marble" dadoes as well as sculptured, painted plaster forms completed the artificial richness of the villas' interiors.

The furniture of the Renaissance, as well as its cabinetry, was most often made of walnut, and this rich brown wood was sometimes enriched by the use of small ivory inlaid patterns and by painted and gilded ornament.

Textiles used for upholstery and draperies were usually made of silk, their patterns being large and colorful. Dress velvets, made in Genoa, were often used for loose cushions and for the upholstery of small pieces of furniture. It is interesting to note that the Italian Renaissance architect (artisan) took the size of a room into consideration when selecting colors. Large rooms received strong colors, smaller rooms softer shades. If neutral-colored plaster walls were used, accessories and draperies were usually brightly colored. In addition to natural colors, the colors used in ancient Greece, Rome, and Egypt continued to be used. These were changed and modified, however, so that, for instance, the scarlet used in ancient Greece became a yellower "pompeii red." Bluish reds appeared. Some gold became rich golden yellow and reddish browns became yellower browns. Generally speaking, the colors used in this period were brown, blue green, a medium greenish blue, a brilliant medium red, and, of course, gold.

This was the period that saw the construction of St. Peter's in Rome (1506–1626) and such other masterpieces as the Gardens of the Villa d'Este at Tivoli (1549). It was the age of Michelangelo Buonarroti (1475–1564), Luca della Robbia (1400–1482), Leonardo da Vinci (1452–1519), Raphael (1483–1520), and Titian (1477–1576). It was, of course, an age of color.

The Flemish Renaissance

While the Renaissance was maturing in Italy in the fifteenth century, its effect began to be felt in all parts of Europe. Each area changed it as it assimilated it. Flanders, a trading station and typical medieval city, was a meeting place for people from all parts of the world at that time. Because of its wealth, art developed at a great pace, and public buildings and private houses were frequently adorned with statuary and carved work, much of which was gilded and colored. Windows were often made of stained glass, and paintings and tapestries were in abundance. One of the greatest contributions made to the arts by Flanders was its establishment of guilds. The painters' guild, for instance, taught the necessary skills to apprentices, who later became journeymen, then masters. The guild obtained commissions for its members and inspected their work, passing upon the honesty of materials and workmanship.

The buildings of Flanders in the fourteenth and fifteenth centuries were Gothic in design and therefore lacked large wall surfaces. The paintings, consequently, were mostly miniatures and illuminations, and the only large-scale use of color occurred in the making of windows. In the fifteenth century, however, large paintings were executed by the van Eyck brothers (Jan, 1385–1440, and Hubert, 1370–1426). Their works, painted in oils, included brilliant colors as well as gold and black. The colors have held up extraordinarily well. Although they did not invent the medium of oil the van Eyck's efforts produced better results than had been obtained previously. Tapestries, too, grew larger and more complicated; they became more brilliant and colorful as the invention of new dyes produced intermediate tones.

The English Renaissance

Because England was a seafaring nation, color was liberally borrowed from many lands. During the Early Renaissance period (1500–1660), color was limited to the use of stained glass and several kinds of wood, including oak. Those walls which were not paneled were sometimes covered with rough-finish plaster. Exposed ceiling beams were sometimes carved and painted, as were plaster ceiling patterns.

During the reigns of Henry VIII and Elizabeth, trading ships brought Chinese pottery and procelains, Turkish rugs, and hand-painted tree-of-life cottons from India. Lighting fixtures were of brass, silver, and wrought iron. Long velvet hangings were frequently used around beds to ensure warmth and privacy.

During the English Restoration (1660–1689) the walls of most rooms continued to be paneled. The wood, walnut or oak, was usually left in its natural state but was sometimes marbleized. Less expensive woods such as pine and fir were often grained to imitate walnut. Olive-wood ornamentation and moldings were often gilded. In the absence of wood paneling, walls were covered with damask or velvet. English and French tapestries were hung in places of importance. Parquet floors of ebony and oak were used, and over these were placed Oriental rugs. It was during this period that Sir Christopher Wren's St. Paul's Cathedral (1668–1670) and St. Mary-le-Bow Church (1680) were constructed in London.

Wall-hung framed paintings and mirrors appeared in the eighteenth century. Colored marbles such as white Siena and dark green verde antique were frequently used for fireplace mantels. Natural-finish knotty pine was used for wall panels, and flock wallpaper, an inexpensive substitute for Italian cut velvet, was introduced. Wallpapers imitating marble and tapestry were also used, and by the middle of the century scenic and pictorial Chinese-inspired papers began to appear. Upholstery included leather and textiles.

The reign of William and Mary (1689–1702) is known as the Age of Walnut, while mahogany was introduced as a cabinet wood during the reigns of Queen Anne (1702–1714) and George I (1714–1727). Furniture was sometimes painted with Chinese or Japanese lacquer. The last part of the eighteenth century and the beginning of the nineteenth are sometimes called the Age of Satinwood because of the introduction of this wood by George Hepplewhite.

The manufacture of colorful and decorative fabrics such as damasks, brocades, velvets, crewel embroideries, brocatelles, and needlepoint reached a high point of development in the skill of the Huguenots, who were forced to leave France because of religious persecution. At the end of the seventeenth century chintz began to be used decoratively.

After the middle of the eighteenth century, plaster often took the place of wood paneling for rooms, and while occasionally these walls were painted a pale color, they were just as often painted white.

The period of the Late Renaissance (1750–1830) in England, including Middle Georgian (1750–1770), Late Georgian (1770–1810), Regency (1810–1820), and Victorian (1837–1901), produced artists whose influence survives today. Thomas Chippendale, George Hepplewhite, Thomas Sheraton, and the Adam brothers (Robert, 1728–1792, and James, 1730–1794) were responsible for the development of some of the finest rooms of the period. They strove for a unity of effect, designing all parts to blend into the whole, both exterior and interior. The rooms were large and formal and were greatly influenced by classic forms found during the excavations then going on at Pompeii and Herculaneum. Wood-paneled walls gave way to plaster decorated with plaster ornament, and moldings. The walls were often painted in pale tones of green, ivory, gray, yellow, and blue; the deeper colors were sparingly used. The Adams used many different shades of green. White marble or plaster figures were often set in niches, crystal chandeliers glittered in the ceilings, and furniture was covered in satins and damasks. The refinement and dignity of these rooms are a high point in design.

It was not long, however, before this style declined into the Regency period with its heavy hand and heavy colors. The development of machines to take over the work of the craftsmen began. During the Victorian period industrialized

England produced an incredible variety of gingerbread ornament and objects. All available space was covered with objects of every sort. Colors were most often heavy and dull, with mauve and purples very popular. Although cream and buff appeared occasionally, by the end of the period, popularly referred to as "The Mauve Decade," there was a wide use of depressing taupes, grays, and browns.

The French Renaissance

At a time when the Renaissance was beginning in Italy, France was consolidating its country after numerous invasions. Gothic art and architecture were declining, and France was ready for a change. The rulers of France, beginning with Charles VIII (r. 1483–1498), were aware of the richness of Renaissance art in Italy and contrasted it unfavorably with their own relatively barren castles. Wars between Italy and France, and subsequent "victories" by France, resulted in the importation of Italian craftsmen. The Renaissance in France dates approximately from the reign of Francis I (1515–1547), who was held prisoner in Italy after a military defeat. During his incarceration he became aware of the rich colors and interior designs of the Italian buildings and brought this interest back to France with him. Henry II (r. 1547–1559) married Catherine de Medici, who continued the introduction of the Italian arts to France. Henry IV (r. 1589–1610) was instrumental in creating religious tolerance in France, and this attracted many Protestant craftsmen from the Low Countries.

Under Louis XIV (r. 1643–1715) France attained a high level of decorative splendor, and French taste was soon accepted as the standard throughout Europe. However, political mistakes, in addition to huge sums spent on costly displays, parties, and amusements, depleted the French treasury and impoverished the people of France. The regency established during the childhood of Louis XV (r. 1715–1774) could do little to improve the economic condition of France, and when he came to the throne, he joined in the luxurious and extravagant life of the court. Louis XVI, weak and impulsive, ruled at a time when France had lost its American colonies and the respect of the rest of Europe. Several years after the French Revolution began, he was executed. The subsequent Directorate (1795–1799) did little to enrich the art of the country, and it was not until Napoleon was proclaimed consul that further progress was made in improving the arts. The aristocracy, who had been responsible for the luxury and refinement of French architecture and interiors, had fled to other countries, and during Napoleon's empire a much less sophisticated style appeared for a much less sophisticated clientele. The Empire period lasted from 1804 to 1814.

The interior architectural spaces of the French Renaissance were large and dark, and walls were usually hung with Gothic tapestries or painted in patterns. Some Gothic wood paneling was used, and structural ceiling beams were often painted. Under Henry II the coffered ceiling panel came into use, and marble-patterned papers were used on walls. During the reigns of Henry IV and Louis XIII, palace rooms became larger and more formal. As the people turned away from the church toward more worldly interests, châteaus and civic buildings received more attention. Wood wall panels became larger and moldings heavier.

The fields of these panels were often painted with patterns borrowed from Spain and Italy. They were almost never left in a natural finish. Moldings were grained and gilded on an off-white background. Floors were occasionally of oak parquet or black-and-white marble and were sometimes covered with Aubusson tapestry rugs or Savonnerie pile rugs in colors that harmonized with the rooms in which they were used. Ceiling coves were occasionally painted with ornament, and the centers of ceilings were often painted with scenes depicting angels and other heavenly beings. Although the rooms of the early Renaissance châteaus did not contain much furniture, that which was used was heavily built and Gothic in feeling. Walnut, oak, and ebony were used for variation in color. Finer furniture was carved, or inlaid with woods of contrasting colors or with bronze, which was sometimes set with semiprecious stones. Upholstery included needlework, velvet, leather, and damask.

It was during the reign of Louis XIV, who determined to make his court the most imposing in Europe, that work was started on Versailles, with its formal gardens and magnificent fountains. Leaders in the fields of architecture, sculpture, painting, and the other arts, as well as craftsmen to execute their designs, were gathered from all parts of Europe to carry this program forward. The conception and execution were of great formality with an extravagance of detail. Rooms were large, with large-scale furniture; curves formed by the compass were used abundantly. Furniture frames, heavily carved, were of ebony, oak, sycamore, chestnut, walnut, and other more exotic woods. Marble was a favorite for table tops. Upholstery included damasks, velvets, leather, needlepoint, cane, and tapestry. Although colors such as blue and gray were inclined to be bright and strong, there was a gradual development of the lighter tones of gray green, gray blue, beige, and pale cream.

As women began to take a more active part in life at court, their influence was also felt in decoration. Furniture, colors, and other aspects of interior design became thinner, lighter, and more feminine. When her influence became very strong during the reign of Louis XV, Madame de Pompadour spent a great deal of time furthering the arts. It was through her efforts that royal societies and patronage for the porcelain factory at Sèvres were advanced, and it was at Sèvres that new chemicals were developed to produce the gold, rose, and king's blue for which this factory became famous. Madame de Pompadour also became interested in Oriental art, and designs with Chinese motifs were developed for use in interiors. It is interesting to note that Chinese hand-painted wallpapers of the time could be imported for less than French artisans charged for making them. Wallpaper was so admired by the middle classes that facilities for its manufacture were set up by Jean Papillon at the end of the seventeenth century.

Textile patterns used for draperies became smaller around this time, and printed cottons in large repeats in red, eggplant, green, and blue, printed on white grounds by the hand-blocked process, became popular. Colors became pale, and neutral hues were used.

Marquetry was very popular in furniture; and in addition to oak, cherry, apple, mahogany, and pear, tulipwood, violetwood, kingwood, and amaranth were used. All these woods were decorated with gold ormolu. In many cases, furniture was also painted in light shades of cream, sky blue, gray, rose, and

7. Kitchen renovation for Mr. and Mrs. Young

James Damico, Architect, Waterbury, CT
Frederick E. Paton, Photographer

(a)

(b)

8. Braniff International terminal, Dallas/Fort Worth Airport
   (a) Waiting area
   (b) Entrance to check-in counter

Harper & George, Designers, New York, NY
George Cserna, Photographer

9. Showroom, High Point, North Carolina

Elroy Edison, A.S.I.D., Designer
Selig Manufacturing Company, Inc.,
Leominster, MA
Darwin Davidson, Photographer

10. "Flotte Française" hand-painted scenic wallpaper

Louis W. Bowen, New York, NY

apricot. Furniture was upholstered in cane, taffeta, brocade, needlepoint, damask, leather, and *tiole de Jouy*.

During the reign of Louis XVI, paneling was not usually carved, and the panels were often painted a plain color or decorated with landscapes and the like. Sometimes textiles were applied. Wallpaper was also used to cover wood panels on plaster walls in simple rooms. Except in the most elaborate rooms, ceilings were merely painted, but in the formal rooms they were decorated to imitate the sky. Furniture was made of mahogany and often painted. Japanese black-and-gold lacquer was substituted for the brighter Chinese types. The colors of materials used for upholstery tended to be light and feminine. Marie Antoinette used smaller rooms as a means of escape from the astonishingly large *salons* of the time. Although the Petit Trianon (1762–1768) was built in the gardens of Versailles during the reign of Louis XV, it has become more closely associated with the name of Marie Antoinette and the trend toward decoration on a simpler scale. Pastel shades of green, yellow brown, pink, chartreuse, and gold became popular.

During the reign of Napoleon, two young architects, Percier and Fontaine, whose taste resembled that of the Adam-period designers in England, set the style of the day. Walls were not often paneled with wood but were hung with wallpaper or textiles and sometimes painted with Pompeian figures. Drapery fabrics were in heavy silk with strongly contrasting colors. Emerald greens, royal purples, brilliant yellows and blues, and wine red formed the spot patterns, which featured victory shields, bees, rosettes, and the letter N. The cabinet-makers attempted to alter their styles, but although they managed to produce furniture of good lines and proportions, economic factors lowered the quality of construction, and the amount of ornament was decreased. Gradually the pieces became heavy and ungraceful. After Napoleon's defeat at Waterloo, the Empire style slowly declined and was finally destroyed by machine production.

THE UNITED STATES

At a time when travel, even for short distances, was exceedingly difficult, settlers came to America from England and developed colonies in Virginia and New England. Unquestionably, the Virginians were different in background from the New Englanders. Many of those who settled in Virginia had lived with the highly developed color schemes that they knew in England. The New England colonials were, for the most part, from a less affluent background. It is only natural that more highly developed and elaborate homes were built in the South, where land had been given by royal grant and where luxuries could be imported. In the early days at least, the less wealthy people of New England, who had a harsher climate to deal with, lived with the bare necessities of life. These did not include elaborate homes or richly furnished interiors.

In New England walls were for the most part white or off-white. Colorful carpet in patterns of oranges, whites, and greens covered the floors. Bedspreads were white or colored. Printed cottons were used for upholstery. The colors of these cottons included mustard yellows, reds, white, and combinations of green, red, and yellow. During the pre-Revolutionary period, when Captain's Houses were very popular, color in New England became heavier in tone and patterns were used. Cotton fabrics with off-white backgrounds were often seen patterned with muted golds and with yellow flowers and green leaves. By and large, the period is marked by a certain practical charm owing to its correct use of color and texture.

Between 1666 and 1720, political conditions in England quieted down, and the American settlers were able to concentrate on enriching their surroundings. By the beginning of the eighteenth century it was obvious that the colonies in America were becoming successful, and this drew additional settlers, including craftsmen such as cabinetmakers and carpenters.

The Georgian look that gave the eighteenth century an elegant quality was greatly influenced by the work of Sir Christopher Wren (1632–1723). It is said that many of the designs of Colonial Williamsburg and of such plantation houses as Carter's Grove were developed by him. The colors used in interiors became stronger. At Carter's Grove one finds large-patterned red and white draperies, red and golden-yellow walls with bright red curtains and upholstery, and red walls with white trim. In the smaller rooms the colors were more muted: Grayish wainscots and trim were set off with red curtains. Often upper walls were white with brightly colored curtains. Often, too, the trim was white, and subdued blue and white wallpaper was used. In another interesting combination, walls and trim were painted a soft, pale gold, with chair seats a bright golden yellow to set off the mahogany furniture and Oriental carpet. The dark mahogany furniture and the deep reddish-brown floor completed the picture. Woodwork was most often painted a color contrasting with the walls, but occasionally they were both the same color.

By the middle of the eighteenth century, the colonies had developed to the point where they could be more heavily taxed by England, and this precipitated the Revolution. The period following the Revolution was one in which certain men, such as Franklin, Hamilton, Jefferson, and Washington, who prided themselves on their knowledge of the arts, not only began to construct more elaborate structures with refined interiors, but, by their example, encouraged the people in the colonies to again look toward Europe for architectural examples.

By the end of the eighteenth and the beginning of the nineteenth centuries, a number of fine examples of post-Colonial architecture began to appear. The inspiration came in great part from ancient Greece and Rome. Although the doors and trim of many buildings of this era were white, the walls were often covered with elaborate paintings and with wallpaper in flowered or diamond patterns; and the rugs, which had been quiet in pattern and color, suddenly became larger-patterned and used brilliant pinks, blues, and yellows. Often, too, the colors of the draperies were bright. In the beginning, New England colors were quieter and more closely related than in later periods.

Williamsburg's interiors were notable because of their restraint and good taste. Few colors were used, but these were employed to accentuate the correctly detailed classic interior spaces. Among the papers of William Allason, a late-eighteenth-century wholesale merchant of Falmouth, Virginia, we find an invoice for such items as linseed oil, fig blue, one barrel of lampblack, one cask of spanish-brown paint, one cask of white lead, and prussian blue. While pigments, especially the ochres and reds, were used in their pure form in many instances, many different hues were obtained by mixing the pigments and by introducing lampblack. All details of these interiors were elegant, and the use of colors was carefully limited: One high color note was used, and all other color elements in the room were subservient to it. Great attention was given to the correct proportion of each color and to the proper amount and disposition of each. In effect, the rooms became three-dimensional paintings.

It is natural that color used in the United States should reflect the national origins of its settlers. Since most of this country's original settlers came from England, early color was indeed English, but even here there was a difference depending upon locale, background of population, and affluence. The settlers in Williamsburg were familiar with the fine English architecture of that time and reproduced it to the best of their considerable ability. Paint colors were made with imported pigments, and many delightful hues were mixed from them. Northern English settlers, less affluent, had to be content with little or no color. Similarly, but on a much smaller scale, the Dutch, French, Swedes, and Germans influenced the areas in which they settled, each group using color in the same way that it had been used in their part of Europe.

The post-Colonial period, particularly the end of the eighteenth and beginning of the nineteenth centuries, produced many fine Greco-Roman buildings in the United States. English colors, together with some from France and some borrowed from ancient times, were popular. A rather bleak period followed, lasting roughly until the Centennial Exposition, which was held in Philadelphia in 1876. This event coincided with a desire for rich surroundings on the part of many *nouveaux riches* in New York, Newport, Chicago, and elsewhere. In order to obtain an aura of culture as quickly as possible, they commissioned their architects to build imitation châteaus and palaces which were copied from those in Europe. Although many celebrated edifices arose, the ordinary individual contented himself with the fussy, ornate, and tasteless style of the Victorian period. Colors continued to be drab and monotonous; cream and buff were most popular. Upholstery and fabrics in burgundy and bright blue were frequently used.

With the twentieth century came World War I, the airplane, Frank Lloyd Wright, the automobile, and the movement to the suburbs, motion pictures, the International Style, the Great Depression, World War II, the Korean War, and the war in Vietnam, all of which affected the daily lives of the entire population and influenced the manner in which people lived. It was not until the end of World War II that tremendous changes evolved in architecture and the arts to bring us to the challenging situation of today.

THE ORIENT

India

Although there are many different peoples and many different climates in India, religion seems to have overcome these differences and to have determined India's architecture and use of architectural color. While national forces were changing with various religious pressures, foreign influences from the West also made themselves felt. Invasions by the Greeks under Alexander and later by the Sassanian Persians left their marks. During the fifth century, a high degree of excellence in the fields of sculpture and painting was achieved in buildings which were essentially meeting halls. Because most of the early meeting halls were apparently built of wood, they are no longer in existence. In about the year 1001, the Muhammadans had invaded India from the east; by 1526 they had established the Mogul empire, and this was the ruling force in India until the English, Dutch, and French arrived in the seventeenth century. English rule was established in 1818.

Rock-cut churches, temples, and monasteries, and buildings such as the Taj Mahal (which is built of white marble inlaid with precious stones in floral patterns) permit us to see the exquisite use of color by the artisans of this land. Wall paintings of the eighteenth century exhibit the importance of contour; figures, for instance, are suggested but are painted flat. Although no paintings from the middle of the seventh century to the eighteenth century seem to have survived, samples of cotton fabric have come down to us. Weaving was one of the most important crafts in India, and the textiles served not only as material for clothing but for bedspreads, hangings, and other furnishings. The word "chintz" was derived from the native name for this material. These fabrics were decorated by printing and painting. Sometimes colors were painted by hand, while colors such as blue were dyed because this was more permanent. Brilliant colors were often used in the arts of India as well as in its architecture, and these were adapted for use by Westerners.

China

The people of ancient China were interested in natural phenomena such as rain, stars, sky, and wind, and their religion was based upon forces of nature. The individual was subservient to the family, and the customs of previous generations later became the law. Just as the individual was a part of an unbroken chain over the centuries, so each type of architecture, together with its colors, remained constant. This constancy is due to the ritualistic and symbolic use of color. For example, royal buildings were roofed in yellow tile, yellow being the color of the royal family. Other tile colors, such as green or blue, were used according to the rank or social status of the owner. Columns, beams, soffits of roof overhangs, and the interiors of these buildings were carved and richly painted with vermilion and gold. Parts of such areas were often lacquered.

One may again see the importance of color in ritual in the Temple of Heaven, Peking, built during the eighteenth century. The tiles of the temple are a deep cobalt to represent the color of heaven. During spring ceremonies, blue was used throughout the service. There were blue porcelain accessories and blue glass windows, and the worshipers themselves wore blue. In similar fashion, Buddhist pagodas were sometimes faced with glazed tiles in yellow, deep reddish blue, green, and red. Wall paintings, done in a flat, two-dimensional manner, were painted as frescoes, panels, and scrolls. Pictures as we know them did not exist, and the panels and wall paintings were not on display constantly but were brought out for special occasions.

Chinese black ink was used for painting as well as for writing. Paintings in this medium were made on silk and were characterized by their delicacy and soft appearance. Mountain scenery was a favorite subject and was beautifully and creatively composed. The mood was usually calm and peaceful. It is interesting to note that certain formulas, protected by custom, were used even here. Mountains could be drawn in sixteen different ways, each of which was fixed in its characteristics.

Of the minor arts, the best bronzes were made in the early periods. Jade was used for personal ornaments, bells, and decoration. Ceramics were at various times given a greenish glaze or painted with brown, green, and yellow glaze. The color of the ceramic pottery varies according to period. During the Ming dynasty (1368–1644) temple vases were painted with a black background with gold chrysanthemums. During the K'ang-Hsi period (1662–1722) vases were painted bright yellow, green, and brown. In the same period, one may also see french ultramarine blue, white, green, coral, and gold. During the last sixty years of the eighteenth century, coral, blue, green, pink, terra-cotta, and lavender came into use. The vases were in many different shapes and sizes. Westerners are perhaps most familiar with celadon, a soft green color. This color may have been used as an imitation of expensive jade.

Japan

Although Shintoism, whose main tenets are an awe and thankfulness before the forces of nature, has long played an important part in the life of Japan, the most important element in its Japanese culture was Buddhism. By the sixth century, Buddhism had changed Chinese thought and culture and had passed its version of them on to Japan. At first, the art of Japan reflected that of China, India, and Korea. Later, however, these tendencies were assimilated. Buddhist influence came from China in three waves: the first during the reign of Empress Suiko (593–628) in the Asuka period (552–645), the second from Tang China (618–907) during the Nara period in Japan (710–794), and the third from Sung China (960–1280) in the Kamakura (1185–1333) and Ashikagon (1338–1573) periods.

While Japan was absorbing these influences, its political power was slowly taken over by barons who set up a military feudalism. Later, the masses had more political importance, and differences of religion were tolerated. As Buddhism weakened, a democratic art began to develop.

Japanese architecture has always reflected a deep-seated love of nature and a fondness for and understanding of wood, the chief available building material. Early Buddhist temples and monasteries imitated similar large Chinese buildings, and the structural parts of these temples were painted with an orange-type vermilion which is now frequently called "chinese red." The exterior walls were made of plaster painted white and sliding shoji screens. The interiors of the Buddhist monastery were very colorful. A statue of Buddha, painted in gold, was covered by a great canopy; the timbers were painted with blue, green, vermilion, and gold and sometimes lacquered. Later, similar structures became lighter in proportion, and exteriors were of natural weathered wood. The interiors were richly treated, and the ceilings were covered with black lacquer and inlaid with mother-of-pearl, ivory, and silver. Much of the structure below was also in natural wood with portions decorated in chinese red and gold. The whole three-dimensional composition formed a magnificent background for those who used the building.

When built for the shoguns, large buildings such as Nijo Castle (1603) were enriched by magnificent and colorful wall paintings and shoji screens consisting of several hinged panels. The backgrounds of most of these paintings and screens were painted with gold dust, and the scenes painted on them included birds, animals, and landscapes. Although each composition was complete on the panel upon which it was painted, it was also part of a total composition of several panels. For example, a rock painted on one panel of a shoji screen continued on to the next. Only the great artists were allowed to do this work. As in Chinese paintings, large areas and many relatively unimportant elements are omitted from each picture. For example, in a four-panel composition at Nijo Castle, dominance is given to two white-and-green birds perched on top of a colorful, but basically gray, rock. Adjacent panels contain only a continuation of the rock on the left side and a pink flower with green leaves on the right. At the top corner of the right panel, however, green foliage of a large pine tree projects slightly into the panel, while a small portion of the trunk of the pine tree occupies only a small corner of the fourth panel. The trunk and large branch occupy two larger panels above. The colors of these paintings are subtle: The pine foliage is a muted bluish green, rocks are gray with tones of green and red, and the tail feathers of one of the birds are a golden vermilion. Other panels have golden-yellow tigers, slate-blue water, and deep green foliage. Wall panels are separated by wide bands of black lacquer and gold, and shojis are edged with narrow bands of black-lacquered wood. Natural-colored cedar timbers divide the panels above.

The Japanese home, whether large or small, achieves its charm by simple means. The interior of the home is united with the natural world outside by opening shojis onto a view of the garden. Vista is important. Colors of materials which are an integral part of the structure are subtle and are those colors found in nature—natural cedar, blue-gray tile, and stucco. Golden-yellow tatami mats are edged with brown for people of the lowest class or with black for the next highest class; they are patterned if for use in buildings occupied by people of great importance. There is little furniture, since the Japanese prefer to sit cross-legged on the floor at low tables, which are usually chinese red or deep mahogany in color.

The highest color note of such a room is located on the *tokonoma*, or raised area, which is used as a shrine. Here one will find a painted scroll with, for instance, a gray border, picturing a gray and red rooster and blond wood, all framed with a narrow black-lacquered frame. In front of the scroll, flowers of an appropriate color, arranged to complement the entire composition, are placed in a vase or bowl. The tokonoma scroll and flowers are changed for various events and seasons. Interestingly enough, one's guest is seated with his or her back to the tokonoma, since it is there that the guest will look most important and honored!

Although color seems to have been sparingly used in dwellings, it must be remembered that the Japanese are constantly aware of it, if not preoccupied with it. Thousands of years of excellent and colorful Japanese art may be seen in many museums both in Japan and around the world. Most of it has been commendably preserved. The subject matter varies, but it includes buildings; war, rituals; such visitors to Japan as the Portuguese, Dutch, and Americans; daily life; and, of course, the many Japanese rulers. Colors include green, red, gold, blue, chinese red, yellow, and black and white. In all cases the total effect is a calm understatement of the subject. In its highest degree of perfection, Japanese art reaches the exquisite state of design referred to as *shibui*.

TECHNOLOGICAL FACTORS

Colors used in the various periods of human history depended upon their availability. Stone Age painters used minerals such as lime, ochre, manganese, and red iron for pigments. For vehicles they used blood, fats, and milk. In addition to these colors, white and black were used by the Stone Age painters in North Africa. The Egyptian artist used clay, mud, and plant juices. The colors for murals were given an adhesive quality by the use of animal glue, wax, and resins, and those used for vase painting were mixed with casein, egg, rubber, and honey. The Greeks and Etruscans were influenced by the Egyptian painters and used similar materials, adding a few of their own. The painting of interiors was done with tempera (containing pigment and egg, and sometimes rubber, milk, or glue). Chinese and Japanese painters used water-soluble pigments when painting on silk, and lacquer when painting on wood. Indian artists used opaque pigments. Pompeian paintings were made with a palette which included a lake-type pink, brown-red ochre, yellow ochre, veronese-green earth, blue, and white.

True paint is a mixture of a pigment with a vehicle. The fluid portion, the vehicle, carries small pieces of pigment in suspension and binds them, by oxidation and hardening, to the painted surface. "Oil paint" is a paint in which the vehicle is a drying oil (usually linseed oil). Oil paints have been used for protective or decorative purposes since the twelfth century.

Pigments may be classified according to source, hue, or chemical composition. Pigments come from various sources—earth, minerals, vegetables, and animals. In addition, organic and inorganic pigments are made synthetically.

Earth pigments include the ochres, siennas, umbers, and green earth. Ochres vary from yellow through red to brown. Italian ochres which contain more than 50 to 70 percent ferric oxide are called siennas because the largest deposit of this material is at Sienna, Italy. Umber is a natural earth color. The most common type, which comes from Cyprus, is known as raw turkey umber and is a warm reddish brown with a green cast. When it is roasted, it turns reddish brown and is called burnt umber. Vandyke brown comes from a rich brown earth mined near Cologne, Germany. Green earth, also called veronese or tyrolese green, is made from earth rich in iron oxide. Today all earth colors are manufactured synthetically and therefore inexpensively.

A number of pigments exist as minerals in nature. Cinnabar (sometimes called vermilion) was used in ancient China, Greece, and Rome. In Greece and Rome it was so expensive that only the wealthy could afford to use it. In Rome, the amount of raw ore that was imported for processing was limited by law to about 2000 pounds annually. During the eighth century A.D., an Arabian chemist named Geber discovered a way to produce cinnabar synthetically. The mass production of synthetic cinnabar began about 1785.

Blue azurite (mountain blue) and green malachite (mountain green) are copper minerals that were used in paintings in the Orient and in the West until the end of the Renaissance. Natural ultramarine blue was made of lapis lazuli, a semiprecious crystalline mineral. Although it was used for jewelry more than 5000 years ago, it seems not to have been used as a pigment before the beginning of the sixth century. In 1828 an artificial ultramarine was produced and, despite its inferior quality, was more widely used because of its lower cost.

Natural white earths such as chalk, kaolin, barites, and china clay are not usable for mixing with oil because they are not opaque. Instead, today's whites are made of white lead, titanium white, and zinc white.

Of the yellows, chrome yellow, made from lead salt and chromate, was used in the nineteenth century and is still used as a tinting color in today's interior paints. Cadmium yellow ranges in shade from lemon to orange to yellow ochre.

Cadmium red, made of selenium and cadmium sulfite, is brighter and bluer than cinnabar.

A number of green colors, such as verdigris, usually made of some form of copper, were used in ancient times. Others, such as Scheele's green and emerald green, both of which contain arsenic, were used in the eighteenth and nineteenth centuries. About the middle of the nineteenth century anhydrous chromium oxide began to be manufactured commercially, and from it were made the chrome oxide greens, which are olive in shade.

Egyptian blue was made of powdered green glass, but it was difficult to apply, and when prussian blue was discovered in 1704, this largely took its place. Cobalt blue and cerulean blue, both chemically obtained, were first sold during the nineteenth century.

A great many blacks have been available to artists. Lampblack, made of the soot formed by earthenware oil lamps, was used in China as long ago as 1500 B.C. Bistre, a brownish black, is made by burning beechwood, vine black by burning grape husks. Bone black and ivory black are made by charring bones. It should be noted that each type of black has its own cast: Some are bluish, some brownish, some grayish, and some deep black. According to its own qualities, each black will therefore modify or change the color to which it is added.

Madder lake, a red, was formerly made by extracting a substance from the roots of the madder plant. Depending upon the conditions of manufacture, the color varied from pink to purple. Now a more stable madder lake is made from pure synthetic alizarin.

A number of other plants, such as persian berries (yellow and green), safflower (red), foxglove (yellow and red), and brazilwood, were once used to make green, yellow, and red lakes. Carmine, a crimson red used in Europe since the middle of the sixteenth century, is made from female cochineal insects. A number of other colors, used mostly for watercolor painting, were made from such materials as the leaves of certain trees, fruit, and the ink bag of the cuttlefish (sepia).

Since about 1850 most dyes and pigments have been made synthetically. Although these dyes were at first not very lightfast, constant work has made them very permanent. This permanence is due largely to the discovery in 1935 of such phthalocyanine dyes as heliogen green and heliogen blue. Other fast colors include lithol red, permanent red, and sunfast red. Needless to say, artificially made dyes and pigments can be produced less expensively and in greater quantities than those made from natural materials. In fact, modern dyes for fabrics are superior in many ways to those made with the natural materials mentioned above. They have a high penetrating power and brightness of shade when this is desired; They are lightfast and may be easily cleaned. Improvements in quality and constancy and the development of new shades are made possible by the use of photomicrography with infared light. New fabrics present new problems of dyeing, but these are constantly being solved by dye chemists. Colored fabrics, therefore, are more readily available to the masses today. Gone is the dependence upon formulas handed down from parent to child. Similarly, with the fantastic improvement in transportation, dyes and pigments are available to all, regardless of location. In addition, the use of color in other artificial products of construction, including tile, concrete, porcelain, aluminum, vinyl, and plastic, has advanced beyond all expectations in recent years.

SOCIOLOGICAL FACTORS

At the end of the nineteenth century, when the new moneyed aristocracy in the United States commissioned architects to build showplaces copied from those in Europe, many architects found it expeditious to study in Europe—particularly since schools of architecture in the United States were, at that time, either nonexistent or basically schools of engineering. In sharp constrast, the Ecole des Beaux Arts at that time was the keeper of good taste, and Americans clamored to go there to study. By 1870, interest in architectural education in the United States had begun to develop. A number of books on home decoration were produced, and a few schools of art and architecture were formed. Subsequent years have seen them develop and multiply, until today, thanks to our many schools of architecture and interior design, many fine designers are supplied to the market each year.

Today, because of our mass media, particularly architectural and interior-design magazines, there is a greater mass understanding than ever before of the problems of interior design and, therefore, of color. Tastes change and vary, and styles wax and wane. Colors are either "in" or "not in" this year, but whatever else may be said, a broad interest in color exists such as the world has never before seen.

Taste is a personal matter, but our architects and interior designers are its custodians. There are pressures, some natural and others artificial, which cause changes in color styles. Newspaper and magazine articles strongly suggest "colors of the month" or "year" for the homemaker, and these trends are accepted without question by many. Although the homemaker can change color schemes as often as the budget will allow, buildings of a less personal nature must be color-designed for greater permanence. Public, industrial, and commercial structures must be studied carefully, and the many principles which are discussed in this book can be used to obtain more lasting results. While fluctuation and variation can be endured in a domestic environment, it is the task of today's designers to keep this trend in check in other buildings. Certainly no one would want to return to the austerity of Victorian or other times which dictated that walls be green, cream, peach, or whatever. Continued education in the use of color can develop an appreciation of its pleasures and advantages in everyone. The correct use of color in our public, commercial, and industrial buildings will further the education of the general public, and this must be the goal of today's designers.

chapter six

THE
APPLICATION
OF COLOR:
BUILT-IN
MATERIALS

Wall hangings and wall coverings were first used to provide warmth in dwellings which were otherwise stark and cold. The members of the household, of course, produced the wall hangings, and since it took a long time to complete each one, they were few in number. In the machine age, it became possible to produce similar hangings and other interior finishes so cheaply that they could be owned by the masses. Today, ease of transportation and a worldwide market make such materials available to anyone who wishes to purchase them.

The arts-and-crafts movement has never entirely disappeared, but the cost of handmade items is prohibitive to many people. In addition, the supply is, of necessity, small. Frequently handicraft industries are developed because of an abundance of skilled artisans in a given area. Most people, however, have within reach a vast number of machine-made materials which are excellent in quality, inexpensive, and easily obtained and installed.

It is important to note that because the education and taste of architects and interior designers differ, not all of them design in the same manner or believe in the same principles of design. Each of the four "schools" of architecture and interior design listed below has its own characteristic approach to color, but ideas, beliefs, and methods flow back and forth between them:

1. Organic architecture, with purity of treatment and use of materials, as practiced by Frank Lloyd Wright and his followers

2. The modern International Movement, as epitomized by the works of Le Corbusier, Walter Gropius, Ludwig Miës van der Rohe, Marcel Breuer, and their followers

3. Historic purity

4. A combination of modern and historic

Frank Lloyd Wright, who believed that the outside and inside of a house should be "of each other," held that an "organic" building should seem to grow out of the ground, and that building and ground should be obviously related to each other. Similarly, he believed that the textures and patterns of draperies, rugs, and furnishings should be sympathetic in design and finish with the house in which they are placed. He believed that in organic architecture the materials should be used in their original state and should not be changed or modified in appearance by the application of paint, wallpaper, or other covering. He was unalterably opposed to the use of paint for covering wood; he felt that wood should be either unfinished or stained.

The designers of the international style within the modern movement strive for a synthesis of all demands and needs. They seek beauty in discipline, restraint, and the greatest possible refinement of all essential elements. They have broken completely with the past and have developed a new, dynamic style in which the volume of the interior of a building, as well as its exterior, is arranged so that its form and proportions create a coordinated whole. Asymmetry replaces symmetry. Simplification and a general lack of ornamentation, both inside and out, are important hallmarks of this style. Large wall areas, bare of ornamentation, and unbroken expanses of glass are used. Materials are carefully selected so that their beauty and natural qualities are expressed by skillful placement, proportion, and detail.

Generally speaking, furniture and furnishings are simple, functional, and an integral part of the total design. In many cases a building's furnishings are designed by the architect. In the beginning, such designs inspired an interest in architectural circles, and at the Bauhaus, from 1925 to 1928, a group of students began to experiment in the design of machine-made items such as tables, chairs, desks, and lighting fixtures. Many architects (like Marcel Breuer, who had taught at the Bauhaus) experimented later in the United States with the design of tubular metal furniture. Others, like Ludwig Miës van der Rohe, began to design truly exquisite furniture, such as his Barcelona chair (1929). Such were the beginnings of the design of modern furniture.

Designers of the third group use only historic forms and color, while the fourth group combines natural materials, manufactured materials, and modern architectural forms with eclectic patterns and forms. The colors used include pastel shades, medium hues, brilliant hues, and combinations of all three. Color and design are almost always asymmetrical. One or two walls in a room are often painted in deep colors, the remaining walls or parts thereof being constructed of a natural material such as wood or stone, or painted gray or off-white. Accents are often brilliant in hue.

The selection of colors and materials varies with the group a designer finds himself in. A design produced according to the "less is more" philosophy of Ludwig Miës van der Rohe will be completely restrained in the use of color, while an interior in, say, the fourth group listed may include an elaborate and unusual use of color. Most clients will insist on traditional interiors for their homes and contemporary interiors and color schemes for their offices.

Interior finishes can, of course, be simple or elaborate, depending upon the budget, the desire of the client, the requirements of the job, and, possibly, the length of time necessary for delivery. An architect may select a color for the brick in a building, only to find that it cannot be obtained in time. A shade of blue terra-cotta selected from a sample kit may be unavailable because it was discontinued the day before. But no matter what their beliefs or desires may be, architects and interior designers have at their disposal many bread-and-butter colors which are usually available in brick, marble, and the newer materials. The latter, of course, are changed at least once a year. The colors and patterns of most products are selected because they appeal to the majority of people, but many special colors originally developed for custom projects eventually become widely popular. Many of the synthetic materials achieve their initial popularity as inexpensive substitutes for expensive natural materials. With refinement and the development of a good color line these materials often attain a beauty and popularity of their own.

Regardless of what materials are used in any given design, success depends upon the proper relationship of parts as well as the correct selection of materials and colors for interior finishes. By thinking of an architectural space as a work of art through which people can walk, we realize that, even if the proportions of the room are correctly established and a sufficient amount of light is provided, correct materials, colors, and textures must be selected and strategically arranged so that the space is united and possesses harmony and balance. Color, materials, textures, and form must be brought together in such a way that they relate to each other without competing and are pleasant to be near. Just as human beings can be related to the height, width, and length of an architectural space by careful use of scale and proportion, so can they be related to the space by carefully locating just the right amount of color used so that each part becomes a successful portion of a pleasing whole.

The art of creating such a pleasing whole is called interior design. Just as a thorough knowledge of its grammar is essential to the mastery of a foreign language, so must one know available materials and their colors in order to be a successful designer. Much of the remainder of this book, therefore, is devoted to an overview of these materials.

FLAME RETARDANCY

In the United States, codes have been developed by governmental authorities or trade or testing organizations to determine the safety of products in many areas, and great attention is paid to flame retardancy. These standards are based on criteria set up by professional scientists and engineers, and tests are performed under specified controlled conditions. The tests are designed to compare the results of the performance of a particular product to a standard. With regard to fire protection, most tests are designed to determine how easily the product will burst into flame; how much the product will add to the fire, and how long it will smolder; what the smoke density will be; and what toxic gases will be produced.

Some such codes are the Boston Code, the New York Port Authority NYPA 701 Code, and the Department of Commerce DOC-191-53 Class 1 Upholstery Burning Test.

It is wise when designing in color to keep in mind the flammability of the material. It is usually possible to check flammability information of any product for an interior space, most especially in contract work, for this information. Various tests, standards, ratings, and codes are presently in effect, and new developments appear constantly. Many manufacturers include this information in their sales literature, and normally they specify flame spread, fuel contributed, and smoke developed. Many times the sales information states that the product is "U.L." rated, which means that Underwriters Laboratories, Inc., of Northbrook, Illinois, has performed tests on it. As the details of this subject are most complex, constant research is required from such organizations as the Office of Flammable Fabrics, National Bureau of Standards (Washington, DC 20237); Consumer Product Safety Commission (Washington, DC 20207); and trade organizations such as the National Association of Furniture Manufacturers, (Washington, DC 20015), the Man-Made Fiber Products Association (Washington, DC 20036), and the National Fire Protection Association (Boston, MA 02110).

WALL COVERINGS

Paint

There are two basic kinds of paint: true paint, which is a mixture of a pigment with a vehicle (the fluid component; see page 63, "Technological Factors"), and varnish, which contains no pigment. Generally speaking, each type of true paint may be obtained in various finishes, as follows:

> *Flat*—used on most wall surfaces
> *Semigloss*—sometimes used for trim
> *Eggshell enamel*—used for trim

In addition to the above there are hundreds of paints available for special uses, such as fire-retardant paint, high-gloss finishes, underbody, primer, rust inhibitor, and waterproof, all available in various colors. There are also stains manufactured in assorted colors. The technology of current paint formulation is most complex. Certain terms, however, are commonly used to describe paint, and these usually refer to the vehicle employed. For instance, oil, alkyd, and epoxy paints employ solvent-type vehicles. Acrylic, polyvinyl acetate, or vinyl acrylic paints contain water emulsion vehicles and are popularly referred to as "latex."

Due to the wide range of prices in paint and the selection of colors, it is wise to use as guidelines such qualities as hiding property and covering quality, length of wear, washability, and easy clean-up.

Ready-mix paints may be obtained in any paint store; the colors available may be seen in color displays, books, or charts. Most paint retailers handle more than one line and quality of paint. Some colors are factory mixed, and while generally true in color they may occasionally vary from the sample chip and from lot to lot. Other colors are mixed in the store by using special formulas and machines furnished by the manufacturer to the retailer. The colors and tints produced are exceedingly accurate.

Martin Senour's Colorobot™ Mark II Color Mixer uses a system developed from ten colorants. By simple punch-card operation almost anyone can process over 2000 colors in any quantity. It has an additional feature called a "customizer" which enables the operator to tint a color to a special tint and have a record of the tint. Similar systems have been developed by other paint manufacturers; examples are Pratt & Lambert's Calibrated Colors System, Benjamin Moore's Moor-O-Matic, and Pittsburgh Paints' DesignaColor System.

The range of ready-mix colors available varies from manufacturer to manufacturer. Benjamin Moore offers over 1400 colors in its Moor-O-Matic System, Martin Senour has 1500 in its Life-Style System, Pratt & Lambert has 937 in its Calibrated Color System, and Pittsburgh Paint, in its DesignaColor System and Manor Hall collection, has a total of 975, in addition to over 1000 colors which were formerly in their line and can still be made available.

The colors shown in manufacturers' books and displays are selected and arranged in different ways. Most firms have many sales tools to assist consumers in determining color selections. In addition, a small group of perhaps twelve to fourteen colors are selected from among the entire line to be promoted during a given season. In addition, such specials as "House and Garden" colors, which are produced each year and are available through many paint manufacturers, provide inspiration for color problems. For the professional, however, where the need for color extends over a great range, there are complete color books or libraries available from the manufacturers of the various paints.

Pittsburgh Paints uses the DesignaColor System, which was created by choosing 120 deep tones from the color spectrum to produce sixteen color families around the color spectrum and six families of neutrals. Within each family clear and muted tones are alternated, and there are five visual progressions from dark to light, or thirty-six colors in each family, for a total of 792 colors. The "chip" album is arranged with the colors as follows:

Reds and pinks	Bright greens	Off-whites
Corals	Gray greens	Pale pastels
Orange	Green tones	Tan tones
Earthy oranges	Blue greens	Browns
Golds	Green blues	Neutrals
Yellows	Blues	Grays
Olive golds	Blue violets	
Yellow greens	Purple	

Benjamin Moore's Moor-O-Matic Library of Colors consists of five looseleaf volumes containing sheets of color perforated in swatch size for use in the preparation of color presentations. The volumes contain the following color categories:

VOL. 1: Yellow, orange, orange-red
VOL. 2: Red, red-purple, blue
VOL. 3: Blue-green, green, yellow-green
VOL. 4: Off-white, neutral
VOL. 5: Toned colors

Finneran & Haley offers 1440 custom colors and 200 standard colors, with 50 Super Colors for accent. They offer a color deck which shows the name and number of the various shades available. The deck is 2 inches wide and 11¾ inches long, with eleven color swatches per sheet. The colors are arranged as follows:

Neutrals	Orange
Blue	Red-orange
Blue-green	Red-violet
Green	Violet
Yellow-green	Blue-violet
Yellow	Deep tones

Some paints are designated by name and number and others by number alone. The light reflectance is indicated by some manufacturers, and this is a great convenience in designing.

The following is a random selection of comparable colors from three manufacturers. Most colors vary from one another in hue, value, or chroma. Sometimes the difference is very slight, occasionally quite marked. Only rarely is there a perfect match.

Color	Finneran & Haley	Pittsburgh	Benjamin Moore
Yellow	620W Irish Linen	P-2272 Yellow Red	1–57
Yellow-green	598M Hay Day	P-2334 Golden Wheat	2–11
Green	354A Holly Wreath	N-7392 Dandelion Greens	12–8
Blue-green	221M Button Wood	M-3005 Troll Green	11–42
Blue	109W Allure	P-2063 Blue Dawn	9–18
Blue-violet	1219W Mellow Mauve	P-2103 Lavender Cloud	7–50
Violet	1166W Lillium	P-2125 Bouquet Orchid	7–10
Red-violet	1062D Roseberry	M-3129 Geisha	6–48
Red (pink)	963M Cinderella Pink	M-3155 Confetti Pink	5–28
Red-orange	896M Sunset	M-3183 Apricot Lily	5–15
Orange	784-M Sunrise	P-2212 Organdy	3–58
Yellow-orange	741M Pineapple Orange	M-3219 Orangeade	3–15

In spite of the efforts of paint manufacturers to supply the needs of the professional with the colors most likely to be required, there are times when colors must be mixed at the job. The following are Universal Tinting Colors which are available for this purpose:

Finneran & Haley	Pittsburgh	Benjamin Moore
Light Yellow	Hansa Yellow No. 1	Permanent Light Yellow
Medium Yellow	Chrome Yellow Light No. 31	Permanent Medium Yellow
Hansa Yellow	Chrome Yellow Medium No. 33	Deep Orange
Chromium Oxide	Medium Yellow No. 13	Permanent Medium Green

Finneran & Haley	Pittsburgh	Benjamin Moore
Thalo Green	Yellow Oxide No. 2	Permanent Red
Thalo Blue	Venetian Red No. 7	Royal Purple
Ultra Blue	Molly Orange No. 20	Thalo Blue
Burnt Umber	Permanent Scarlet No. 21	Raw Sienna
Raw Umber	Bulletin Red No. 14	Burnt Sienna
Burnt Sienna	Permanent Red No. 17	Venetian Red
Raw Sienna	Permanent Violet No. 36	Burnt Umber
Yellow Oxide	Thalo Blue No. 11	Raw Umber
Thalo Red	Permanent Green Light No. 8	Tinting Black
Venetian Red	Permanent Green Medium No. 9	
Toluidine Red	Permanent Green Dark No. 10	
Molly Orange	Thalo Green No. 12	
	Chromium Oxide No. 15	
	Raw Sienna No. 18	
	Burnt Sienna No. 5	
	Burnt Umber No. 4	
	Raw Umber No. 3	
	Lamp Black No. 16	

All the above colors are deep in tone and, of course, can be lightened by adding white. When lightening a color, however, remember that since white contains a great deal of blue, it not only lightens but also changes some colors. For example, vermilion when lightened with white turns to vermilion pink, and chrome yellow orange turns to orange pink.

It is important, too, to remember that yellow ochre and raw sienna, while they look somewhat alike, are different and affect other colors differently. Furthermore, while most colors are readily identifiable by name, the earth colors are not, and they should be memorized. When lightened, raw sienna is gray yellow, burnt sienna is gray pink, burnt umber is pinkish brown, and raw umber is a warm neutral gray. Black, when lightened, becomes bluish gray.

Finally, it must be said that the tinting colors listed above will not give you every color you want. There will be times when you will have to buy tubes of artists' oil colors to get the proper results, but this should be considered only after all available universal tinting colors have been examined.

Compare the splendid list of colors at our disposal today, however, with the few that were available to, say, the architects of colonial Virginia. Some of these were fig blue, lampblack, spanish brown, prussian blue, yellow ochre, white, and red. But while the paucity of colors limited the architect, a great variety of hues resulted from the mixing of the several pigments.

In order to supervise the painter in the mixing of special colors, architects and interior designers must know how to mix color. Not only must they know the basic principles of color theory (see Chapter 1), they must also be able to analyze visually any color they are trying to produce so that they will know what tinting colors should be used to obtain the desired results. Ideally, the novice should experiment with the mixing of colors by using white paint and tinting colors. If this is impractical, it is possible to obtain similar results using tempera colors, as they react in a way almost identical to alkyd paints. Tempera will dry more quickly than oil, but experimentation using small wash dishes will save a great deal of time and money and give the novice good practice in the art of mixing paint.

Paint samples should always be made by first introducing a small amount of white paint in a white wash dish, then introducing small amounts of color. (If you begin by introducing colors in a wash dish, and then add white, you will soon have more paint than you require.) The same procedure should be followed when mixing paint for a job: For example, start with white and carefully add tinting color. As mentioned above, the addition of white to a color does not automatically produce a lighter shade; sometimes the color becomes chalky and unrelated to the original color. In the same way, the addition of black to a color does not automatically darken the color, because black contains a great deal of blue, and it often changes the color. Many interesting phenomena may be observed by mixing various colors together. Black and yellow make green, for example, and black and certain types of green make a soft shade of blue! Mixing colors is an enjoyable and rewarding process. It is wise to use small quantities of paint for the initial paint samples so that experimentation does not spoil large amounts of paint.

Small white index cards should be kept handy for trying out the colors and allowing them to dry. Sometimes changes will occur in the drying process, and you may want to compensate for these. Another word of caution: In mixing paints on a job, you will find that painters use different brands of white. These will vary from a gray white to a pink, yellowish, or bluish white. Obviously, if a color is not to have any pink in it, white containing pink should not be used. If it is not to have any blue, white without blue should be used.

Restoration Painting

Most paint companies have done a great deal of research to develop colors which may be used in the restoration of historic buildings. Finneran & Haley of Philadelphia have cooperated with the National Park Service in the restoration work done in Historic Philadelphia, which typifies the methods by which original colors are uncovered. For instance, some areas of Independence Hall, upon examination, were found to contain as many as a hundred coats of paint. As the earlier paints contained a great deal of lead, this film was a very thick one. Painstaking research involved the removal of a section of paint film down to the bare wood from a particular location. Under a microscope a portion of each layer of paint film was removed, revealing each successive coat down to the original. Chemical analysis determined the composition of the film. Additional research was done on paint manufacture by checking old bills of sale and referring to advertisements in old newspapers. Paint pigments, oils, driers, and so on were studied.

A comprehensive group of thirty-two colors has been assembled by Finneran & Haley, and the following have been authenticated through the cooperation of the National Park Service as used in Historic Philadelphia buildings.[1]

Constitution Tan	Independence Hall White
Rittenhouse Gold	Independence Hall Ash
Supreme Court Yellow	Congress Hall Red
Todd House Yellow	Liberty Gray
Congress Hall Tan	Long Gallery Blue
Independence Hall Quill	Grand Staircase Blue

[1] Finneran & Haley bulletin.

Other colors in the collection are typical of those used in the East Coast colonies:

Pennfield Brown	Colonial Mauve
Elfreth's Alley Brown	Mt. Pleasant Pink
Battlefield Moss	Flintlock Gray
Sweetbriar Sand	Quaker Gray
Revolutionary Gold	Belmont Blue
Congress Hall Tan	Tower Stair Hall Blue
Cobblestone Ivory	Germantown Green
Lime White	Grovers' Lane Green
Penn Red	Tun Tavern Green
Fort Mifflin Brown	Woodford Green

While these commercial paints with their subdued chroma and earthen pigments are an excellent tool for many projects, the National Park Service, in its desire to restore the buildings for Independence National Park as closely as possible to their original appearance, regarded commercial paints as too fine for their use. Therefore, artisans ground pigment by hand and mixed their own paints to produce the ropey appearance of the original.

Other manufacturers of paint have concentrated on historic districts in other sections of the country. Martin Senour has a collection of Colonial Williamsburg Restoration Paints in eleven colors, each available in four let-downs. Pittsburgh Paint has a selection of forty-four Historic Colors. Many more are available for use in projects of an historic nature.

Wallpaper

Wallpapers were originally a substitute for wall painting and decorative hangings. Their first use seems to have been in China, in small rectangular pieces, and they were introduced to France and England during the seventeenth century. The French worked up a domestic substitute with marble graining and small hand-painted or stenciled patterns. Flocks were imitation brocades and velvets. In the middle of the seventeenth century, Jean Papillon, a Frenchman, carved patterns in wood blocks and used them to produce printed wallpapers. These were the forerunners of wallpaper as we know it today. Later, printed panels replaced hand-painted wall designs. As styles of decoration changed, wallpaper designs were produced to harmonize with these fashions. Scenic papers were printed from about 1800 to 1850 and were very popular in Europe and America. About 1840, machine-printed papers on cheap backgrounds appeared.

Modern wallpapers are available in roller-printed (Figure 6.1a) and hand-blocked designs (Figure 6.1b) and scenic patterns (Plate 10). Because more brilliant accents and subtler shadows are possible in the hand-blocked process, these papers are more beautiful than the machine-printed ones, but they are also more expensive. In addition, the repeat of a hand-blocked paper can be greater than that of a roller-printed paper, since the repeat in the latter is determined by the circumference of the roller. Scenic wallpapers are made in a series of vertical strips that, when hung, form a mural-like wall decoration. Some modern designs are versatile. The designer can arrange the pattern as he wishes. For example, strips numbered 1, 2, 3, and 4 need not be used in numerical order, but may be used in any order desired; the parts may also be used on various walls of the same room.

FIG 6.1   Wallpaper

(a) Roller-printed

(b) Hand-blocked
Katzenback & Warren, Inc., New York, NY

Wallpapers vary in color and pattern from traditional to modern, from realistic to abstract. The grounds upon which wallpapers are printed are available in many colors and shades—white, gold, silver, green, black, blue, amber, yellow, ivory, purple, pink, red, peach, and brown. Patterns are printed in colors which constitute carefully studied color schemes. For instance, a pattern of white and gold may be printed upon a wedgwood blue; or tangerine and brown may be printed on white. Each pattern is usually available in several choices of colors. For instance, one design might be available in the following combinations of colors:

1. Pink, orange, and green on a white background
2. Blue and green on natural grasscloth
3. Blue, green, and yellow on bronze silk

Another pattern might come in the following variations:

1. Brick, persimmon, and yellow green on a white ground
2. Violet, fuchsia, and gold on a white ground
3. Blue and lime on a white ground
4. Curry, orange, and brown on a white ground

If it is difficult to visualize how a color will look in a room, it is doubly difficult to visualize how a colored wallpaper will appear; much study is necessary to develop a knowledge of the effects of different patterns and colors. As large a sample as possible of the wallpaper should be obtained for the preliminary analysis of color, pattern, and scale. A large room will require a pattern containing large elements, and a small room calls for a pattern with small elements. The pattern and color of a wallpaper give a feeling of movement that must be taken into account in the furnishing of the room. Usually a patterned wallpaper will cause a room to appear "busy," so that quietly covered furniture should be used as a complement. A "busy" room also calls for less furniture than a room with walls of solid color. Frequently a single wall is papered, and the remaining walls are painted.

A wallpaper can be obtained for every conceivable room, but what is appropriate in one place may not look good in another. While an entrance foyer may have an overscaled orange-tree pattern to delight the visitor, a bedroom should properly have a relatively soft and quiet paper. A dining area which is relatively small can be given greater depth by the use of a scenic-pattern paper on one wall to give a sense of perspective. The selection of wallpaper should be made with great care to ensure the most effective solution. Today's wallpaper designs vary from geometric to floral, from spot patterns to allover patterns. Modern usage calls for strong, clear colors in abstract patterns. A rose in a modern design, instead of being carefully and realistically delineated, is a splash of color with an irregular outline. Round spots become splashy, irregular shapes in an attempt to relate them to abstract or impressionistic art.

Wallpapers can be treated to make them washable. Sometimes this treatment is included in the manufacturing process; sometimes it must be added when it is purchased. Most wallpaper is sold in rolls containing 36 square feet, but packed in single (36 square feet), double (72 square feet), or triple (108 square feet) roll quantities. In figuring the amount of wallpaper required for a project, it is wise to check the exact size of the paper and the repeat of the pattern before ordering. To ensure a smooth surface, lining paper, a thin, low-cost

FIG. 6.2 Grasscloth

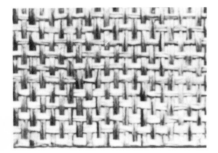

(a) Cellulose horizontal-
    stripe weave

(b) Cellulose herringbone weave

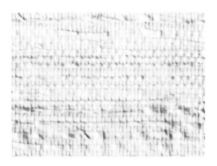

(c) Reed and fine hemp—
    horizontal stripe

(d) Grasscloth
    Scalamandre Wallpaper, Inc.,
    New York, NY

paper, should be hung before the top paper is applied. It is always best to remove old paper before applying the new.

In addition to using conventional wallpaper, it is often possible to laminate a fabric to paper or vinyl for special effects. The work can be done on a custom basis, but there are also available stock patterns of fabric and wallpaper such as those offered by Durawall, Inc., from a collection of the Belgian Linen Association. Patterns include vertical stripes in shades of white, brown, and beige; colored stripes with blues, brown, green, and white; and overall patterns woven with beige and white, brown and tan, green and tan, orange and tan, blue and tan, or light and dark tan. The weights of the patterns range from heavy to fine, and the weaving also ranges from nubby to smooth. The acoustical advantages of using fabric are also a great consideration in this type of installation.

Grasscloth

Grasscloth long handcrafted in Japan, was first used on the walls of Buddhist temples. Since it is for the most part cottage-industry manufactured, it varies in color and texture from roll to roll and lot to lot. But these very variations contribute to its beauty and charm. The "grass" for the basic types of grasscloth is made of fiber taken from the inside of the honeysuckle vine. The raw material is soaked, cleaned, cut to strands of approximately the same width, dyed, woven on hand looms in various patterns, and mounted on thin paper. Although the usual undyed grasscloth varies in color from a brownish beige to a greenish tan, nearly 200 other colors and textures are available. Variations are obtained by including in the weave bamboo, threads, and papers of various colors, such as white, brown, green, yellow, taupe, black, gold, orange, and blue. The fibers of some grasscloth papers are dyed before weaving; these fibers are available in various reds, blues, and greens, and in a relatively muted yellow. Further variations are obtained by employing different types of weaves. The simplest is a basket weave; the more complicated range from linen-type weaves to highly sophisticated chevron patterns (Figure 6.2). In addition, patterns are created by using two or more colors in rectangles, or by combining grasses of several colors and weaving them together with various combinations of regular and irregular stitching. In some designs, bamboo strips of varying widths are woven together in a continuous pattern; in others, they are woven together with grass which has been dyed a contrasting color.

The variety in grasscloth is almost endless. The striped patterns, however, are made to be used horizontally; it is almost impossible to align the pattern of one roll with that of the next. This limitation must be kept in mind. The variations in color and pattern contribute to the beauty and uniqueness of the overall effect, but it must be remembered that there will be unevenness in the continuity of the pattern.

For those who prefer them, there are grasscloths which contain silk, rayon, net, cellulose, and metallic papers, as well as various kinds of reeds. The silks are commonly known as *shikii* silks and are available in exotic iridescent shades.

Grasscloth requires care in application, but it provides no difficulty for the experienced paperhanger. It is available in the usual double roll, which contains about 72 square feet, but there are variations in width according to texture and material, so the dimensions should be verified for each pattern.

FIG. 6.3 Vinyl wall covering

Vinyl

Wallpapers can be given some measure of protection against soiling by the manufacturer or the consumer, but this protection is not always sufficient. In areas where walls will become quite soiled, because of heavy traffic or for other reasons, a heavy-duty covering is required. There is available on the market today a wide range of popular vinyl-coated wall coverings, some paper-backed, others cloth-backed. Vinyl plastic is also available for upholstery, but this section will deal exclusively with vinyl wall covering.

The available patterns have, generally speaking, been inspired by wallpapers, grasscloth, and various fabrics, including silk, linen, and *bouclé*. The designers have also imitated wood, marble, stone, cork, leather, stippled rough plaster, and textured metals (see Figure 6.3). Due to economic factors, no doubt, some patterns are available in only five colors, while others are available in as many as thirty. In many lines, certain of the colors are common to several patterns. But for the most part the color line of each pattern ranges from pure white through pale tones (such as peach, pink, green, blue, and yellow) and medium tones to the darker shades of blue, green, brown, red, gray, and yellow. This variation makes vinyl wall coverings a versatile tool for the architect and interior designer.

(a) Leather pattern

(b) Grasscloth pattern

Vinyl wall coverings vary in weight as well as in color and pattern. The weight should be determined by the use. Most manufacturers provide weight-usage recommendations. The success of a vinyl installation depends upon the skill of the installer, who should be expert in this work. Vinyl must be applied with a special adhesive which is usually sold by the manufacturer who supplies the vinyl.

Over the years, certain vinyls have proved to be more colorfast than others. Those in which the color is an integral part of the vinyl seem to keep their color better, but improvements in this field are being made constantly.

Printed patterns are available in vinyl in both stock and custom designs and colors (see Plate 8). These are surface prints, however, and the designer should realize that some cleansing processes may remove the pattern in a short time. Actual tests, using the exact methods of cleansing that will be employed after the vinyl is installed, should be repeatedly made on samples to determine their durability.

(c) Grass pattern
Vicrtex, L.E. Carpenter & Company,
New York, NY

Vinyl wall coverings come in different weights and thicknesses. The weight of one brand varies from 22.5 to 36.0 ounces per linear yard in the 54-inch width. The thickness varies from 0.021 to 0.035 inches. Weight and thickness alone, however, do not determine how much abrasion a vinyl wall covering will stand. The density and purity of the vinyl mix is also crucial. One of the best-known abrasion tests is the Taber test, and manufacturers' literature should be checked for performance in this test.

Since vinyl wall coverings are frequently installed where fire protection is important, proposed patterns should be examined before they are purchased to make certain that they meet the requirements of local fire codes and authorities. The Underwriters' Laboratory, Inc. tests the flame-spread characteristics, smoke density, and toxicity of vinyl coverings, and manufacturers can supply the test results. It is important that these tests be accepted by all agencies having jurisdiction for use in buildings of various types. In extreme instances, it may be necessary to have special tests made.

Wood

Of all the materials available to the designer of interiors, wood offers the greatest number of possibilities. It can be worked easily, it can be obtained in an almost limitless number of colors and patterns, and it has an inherent beauty that is impossible to match. The general category of woods that the interior designer is interested in is called "hardwoods." It has been said that there are about 99,000 different species of hardwoods throughout the world, but only about 250 are commercially available. Of these, the following are perhaps the best known:

Afromosia	Laredo (breadnut)
Ambera	Laurel, East Indian
Ash, brown	Mahogany, African
Ash, white	Mahogany, Honduras
Aspen	Makore (African cherry)
Avodire	Minzu
Basswood	Maple
Beech, American	Myrtle
Benge	Narra
Birch, natural	Oak, American
Birch, white	Oak, English
Boose (African cedar)	Oak, brown
Bubinga	Oak, red
Butternut	Oak, white
Cedar, aromatic	Orientalwood
Cherry, American	Padouk, Burma
Cherry, foreign	Paldao
Chestnut, English	Persimmon
Chestnut wormy	Pearwood, Swiss
Cypress	Primavera
Ebony, Macassar	Pecan
Elm, Carpathian	Poplar, yellow
Elm, American brown	Rosewood, Brazilian
Gum, red	Rosewood, Madagascar
Goncalo, alves (tiger wood or zebra wood)	Rosewood, East Indian
Hackberry	Sapele
Harewood, English	Satinwood
Hickory	Silkwood
Honey	Sycamore, American
Kmbuya	Sycamore, English
Koa	Tupelo (gum)
Kokrodua	Teak, African
"Korina" (limba)	Teak, Burmese
Lauan, red	Tola
Lauan, white	Tamo (Japanese ash)
Lacewood	Thuya

Tigerwood
Tulipwood
Vermilion
Walnut, American

Walnut, European
Walnut, Rhodesian
Wenge
Yew, English

**THE
APPLICATION OF
COLOR: BUILT-IN
MATERIALS**

81

An examination of various kinds of wood shows a wide spectrum of colors from pale yellow pink through pink and medium pale yellow to brownish orange, pinkish brown, reddish brown, black brown, and almond (see Plate 11). The color varies according to the species. Beauty and additional variation may be obtained in veneers by creating "figure," which is determined by the species of the tree, the cutting method, and the part of the tree from which the veneer is cut (see Figure 6.4).

Plywood is made by laminating three or more layers of wood with adhesives. The face ply is the veneer that is to be seen. The center ply is called the core, and the ply immediately adjacent to the face ply is called a "crossband." Plywood construction may have three, five, seven, or any other odd number

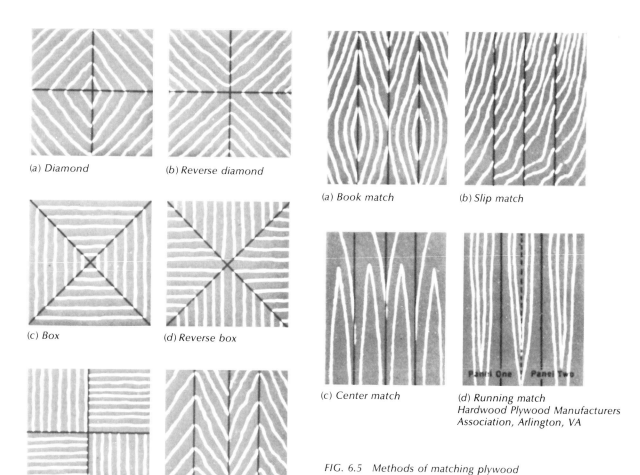

(a) Diamond

(b) Reverse diamond

(c) Box

(d) Reverse box

(e) Checkerboard

(f) Herringbone
Hardwood Plywood Manufacturers
Association, Arlington, VA

FIG 6.4   Different types of matching plywood

(a) Book match

(b) Slip match

(c) Center match

(d) Running match
Hardwood Plywood Manufacturers
Association, Arlington, VA

FIG. 6.5   Methods of matching plywood

of plies. The grain of each layer is laid at right angles to the grain of the adjacent ply. The face ply can be cut in several ways—plain slicing, quarter slicing, rotary, half-round, and rift cut. Depending upon the type of wood used, additional patterns and figures can be obtained. Some of them are listed below (see Plate 12):

Patterns	Figures
Pencil stripe	Stumpwood
Fiddleback	Feather crotch
Mottled	Crotch swirl
Blistered	Birdseye
	Crossfire
	Ribbon stripe

Further variation can be obtained by the manner in which the wood is matched. Veneers may be selected for a particular kind of graining, then joined together within a panel to produce various figures (see Figure 6.5): diamond, reverse diamond, box, reverse box, checkerboard, and herringbone. Book match is obtained by turning over alternate sheets of a flitch in the manner of opening a book. (A flitch is a section of a tree that has been sliced and kept together; more than one flitch can be cut from a large tree.) Slip match is obtained by placing adjacent sheets of veneer side by side without turning. (It is also called slide match.) Center match is obtained by placing an equal number of sheets with the same pattern on each side of a center line. Running match (or lot match) is obtained when veneers are laid up in the same sequence as they occupy in the flitch. Excess veneer from the first panel is used to begin the second panel; excess veneer from the second panel is used to begin the third panel, and so on.

The average woodwork mill stocks a fairly limited number of woods. A number of companies produce stock plywood paneling, which varies in price from inexpensive to moderately expensive. The range of woods available depends on their popularity; only a relatively small number of plywoods can be stocked. Among those most commonly available are birch, butternut, cedar, black cherry, wormy chestnut, mahogany (both African and Honduras), red and white oak, pecan, pine, Brazilian rosewood, teak, and walnut. In addition to natural finishes, a number of "tortured" finishes are available in several colors. These are made by sandblasting the face of the panel, thereby eroding the soft grain and leaving the harder grain in relief.

In addition to the foregoing commercially available plywoods, solid wood panels are also obtainable. They vary in species and grade as well as width and length. The following selections are offered by Townsend Paneling Division of Potlatch Corporation, Stuttgart, Arkansas:

Standard Line	Carriage House Line
Rough-sawn walnut	Cordova oak
Burley pecan	Tostado ash
Colonial ash	Gothic
Delta cottonwood	Viridian oak
Pecky cyprus	
Wattled walnut	
Colonial cherry	
Butternut	
Colonial red oak	

Benchmark walnut
English Channel oak

The architect or interior designer will in most cases wish to select personally the paneling that is to go into an installation. In many cases he or she will be able to see both plywood and solid panels at a local showroom. However, if the job is an important one, the designer will probably visit a showroom such as that of William L. Marshall, Ltd. in New York, where the desired veneer may be selected for length, color, and grain.

Suppose Jane Doe, a designer, wishes to use Brazilian rosewood. In the showroom she will be shown samples of wood from which to make her selection. She will find that most of the color in the wood will vary from yellow to a pinkish gray. Each ply in the bale will be numbered to indicate its relative position in the tree before it was sliced—for example, 1-3, 2-3, or 3-3. As many as eight representative samples will be kept for each flitch. The best wood is cut into veneers, since more good face wood can be obtained from a tree in this manner. Defective wood is sold as lumber.

When the flitches have been selected, they are sent to the plywood manufacturing company. When a flitch has been sold, the sample of it in the showroom is cut for general-use samples to prevent the possibility that it may be shown to another client.

Generally speaking, the flitches shown in the showroom are unfinished, and the finishing process is chosen by the architect or interior designer. However, it is recommended that a material which does not hide the grain (such as water-soluble stains or lacquer) be used rather than oil stains, which tend to hide the grain of the wood.

In addition to the usual methods of using wood, a number of "banded" woods are made by gluing together several plies of two different colors. For example, wood panels made by the "fine-line process," which is popular in Europe, are made by gluing together bands of light and dark plywood sheets. When these sheets have been glued together in a log, they are sliced vertically into panels; the light and dark wood shows as a pattern on the face of each panel. The pattern can be varied as desired by varying the distance between the dark sheets.

With all the different kinds and colors of wood available, the color selection for any given job might seem to be complicated beyond belief. However, the same set of principles described in Chapter 1 on color theory can be used here. Look closely at a piece of walnut, and you will see that it is not all one color, but several colors. The background may vary from reddish brown to yellow brown, while the graining may be blue brown. Therefore it is safe to say that walnut has in it red, yellow, and blue. If the wood has a yellow cast, it is obvious that yellow is one of the colors that may be used with it. Zebrawood falls into this category. An examination will show that it contains yellow (chrome yellow), red (an alizarin crimson), and blue (a french ultramarine). By mixing these three colors, plus white, the color of zebrawood can be obtained. This fact means that any of these three colors may be used alone or in combination in varying amounts to complement zebrawood.

When the color of unfinished teak is analyzed optically, it will be found to contain yellow ochre, vermilion, and cobalt blue. The colors in a pinkish rosewood will be yellow ochre, alizarin crimson, and a french ultramarine blue. If one wall in a paneled room is to be painted, there are several color options. It can, of course, be painted a color similar to the general tone of the wood, in a lighter or darker shade. It may be painted any of the colors that are found in the optical analysis of the wood. A color complementary to the general tone of the wood may be used; for instance, if a wood such as teak has a yellow-orange cast, a shade of blue violet, its complement, may be used with it. Analogous colors, such as orange and yellow, may also be used. One of the triads containing yellow orange may be employed. A good triad would be a scheme of yellow orange, red violet, and blue green, or a split complement using a yellow orange and perhaps a violet and a blue.

Obviously, with the type of expenditure required for the use of an exotic wood brought from some far corner of the earth, color studies illustrating all the colors and textures to be used in the room, as well as a good colored perspective drawing, should be made before any of the materials are ordered.

Plastic Laminates

Of all the plastics that are available to the architect and interior designer, plastic laminates are perhaps the best known and most widely used. Essentially, these are made of extremely hard and durable plastic that is mounted as a veneer on plywood or other board. Used on walls, counters, table tops, furniture, cabinetry, vanitories, and wall panels (see Plates 13a and 13b), they are colorful and durable. Special qualities are produced to be used where the requirements are more stringent than those for residential use; examples are bank or other commercial counters and laboratory cabinet tops, which are subject to attack by chemical substances.

There are several brands of plastic laminate on the market manufactured by firms that are members of the Decorative Laminate Section of the National Electrical Manufacturers Association. Each company has a distinctive selection of colors, patterns, and specialties. The range varies from year to year as new colors are introduced and less active ones are dropped. Different finishes, such as smooth, glare-free, sculptured, or textured, are available to suit special requirements. The finishes offered by Formica are Suede –65, Suede –58, Furniture –30, Polished –90. Wilson Art offers such finishes as Satin, Velvet, Cuero, and Glass. In addition, grades for both horizontal and vertical interior applications are available, as well as "forming grade," which is capable of being bent to a small radius. Vertical grade is engineered for vertical surfaces subject to less wear than horizontal work surfaces.

Widths of 24, 30, 36, 48, and 60 inches and lengths of 72, 84, 96, 120, and 144 inches are generally available, but the selection of sizes in some patterns is limited.

The products of two companies will be described here as representative of the plastic laminates now on the market. Formica offers thirty-six solid colors with several neutrals, a few deep tones, and a pleasant range of yellows, oranges, and greens. Wilson Art Design Group 1 (solid colors) contains forty colors, also with a good range of neutrals, but also several hues of relatively deep intensity.

The solid colors offered by Formica are as follows, and most of them are in Suede –65 Standard Finish:

Brick Orange	Grass Green	Gaelic Green
Sliced Avocado	Tahiti Orange	Ginger Brown
Scarlet	Buttercup Yellow	Black
Harvest Gold	Wheat	Neutral White
Banner Blue	Primrose	Champagne
Pumice	Vanilla	French Blue
Lemon Twist	Desert Beige	Putty Gray
Green Olive	Sand	Antique White
Butterscotch	Cream	Angola Brown
Bittersweet	Toucan Yellow	White
Persimmon	Terra Cotta	Adobe Gold
Poppy	New Celadon	Ice White

Wilson Art offers the following solid colors in their Design Group 1:

Solid White	Bright Russet	Autumn Glory
Solid Frosty White	Burnt Umber	Terra Cotta
Solid Antique White	Sienna	Bittersweet
Light Beige	Dark Bronze	Valencia
Beige	Slate Grey	Sliced Avocado
Putty	Solid Black	Monarch
Morocco Sand	Adobe Gold	Spring Green
Pongee	Ivory Yellow	Vibrant Green
Harvest Gold	Aztec Gold	Olivine
Sierra	Lemon Twist	Powder Blue
Honey	Saffron	Chateau Blue
Inca Gold	Burnt Orange	Persian Blue
Mandarin Red	Tangerine	
Regimental Red	Mission Orange	

Among the Woodgrain patterns, the following are available:

Formica	*Wilson Art, Design Group 1*
Butcherblock Maple	Natural Butcher Block
(Long Grain)	Butcher Block Crossgrain
(Crossgrain)	Mellowed Cherry
Provincial Cherry	Barcelona Oak
English Oak	English Oak
Spanish Oak	Glazed Oak
Natural Oak	Bannister Oak
Shawnee Walnut	Gunstock Walnut
Regency Walnut	Winchester Walnut
African Teak	Danish Walnut
Honeytone Teak	Brown Indian Teak
Cortena Pecan	Amber Teak
Summer Pecan	Cortena Pecan
Gunstock Walnut	Valley Pecan
White Tidewood	Driftwood
Rosewood	Natural Rosewood
Butcherblock Oak	White Rosewood
Wormy Chestnut	Wormy Chestnut
Sun Beech	Timberline
	Natural Random Block Burl

Marble patterns offered are the following:

Formica	*Wilson Art, Design Group 1*
Classic Cremo Marble	Braganzia Marble
Portugese Lioz Marble	Torino Marble
Antique Lioz Marble	Lalique Marble
Norwegian Marble	Roman Marble
	Green Roman Marble
	Blue Roman Marble
	Classic Onyx Natural
	Light Tan Marble
	White Fantasia Marble
	White Slate
	Black Slate

Formica also offers the following Stone patterns:

Ming Onyx	Green Onyx
Regal Jade	Roman Onyx
Regal Topaz	White Onyx
Fire Agate	Persian Onyx

Some classic patterns, in small scale, are offered by Formica in Furniture –30 finish:

Gold Gossamer: Faint gold mottle on white

Avocado Gossamer: Faint avocado mottle on white

Garden Gossamer: Faint avocado and gold mottle on white

Yellow Willow: A series of yellow lines which simulate bare tree branches on white ground

White Sequin: Random flecks of gold on white ground

White Spindrift: Flecks of gold and graining on white ground

Firedance: Faintly mottled pattern in deep orange on orange ground—Suede –58 finish

The range of small-scale patterns available from Wilson Art is as follows:

Gold Fantasia: Medium yellow ground with lighter and deeper shading

Bronze Fantasia: Medium yellow to rust mottled pattern

Sauterne Jade: Yellow-green mottle from deep to light tones

Autumn Sunstone: Medium gold mottled to give a flowery, shadowy effect

Lime Cambay: Pale lime green mottled to give a flowery, shadowy effect

Golden Cambay: Gold mottled as above

Harvest Web: Gold in small chip pattern

Avocado Allegro: White ground with chip pattern outlined in avocado

Harvest Inca: Pale gold faint abstract pattern on white

Avocado Inca: Similar abstract pattern in avocado on white

Avocado Capri: Stone pattern in pale avocado on white

Harvest Capri: Stone pattern in pale shades of gold

Fire Tarantella: Red-orange chip pattern shaded from dark to pale

White Spun Lamé: Random gold flecks and threads on white

White Lamé: Random gold flecks on white

White Neutraltone: Small scale shadow pattern of beige on white

Avocado Vallejo: Random thread pattern of avocado on white

Harvest Mallejo: Paler rendition of above

Harvest Leaves: Leaves of gold on white ground

Misty Tarantella: Gold chip pattern shaded from pale to deep

The following Leather patterns are available:

Formica

Tawny Rawhide
Beige Rawhide
White Kid
Green Leather
Cimmerian Leather
Brown Leather
Gold Leather

Wilson Art

White Leather
Brown Leather
Green Leather
Spanish Leather
Harvest Leather

Formica offers two metallic patterns, Bronze Celestial and Copper Celestial.

Wilson Art offers a line of metallic laminates in bas relief in a variety of abstract pattern and colors, deeply embossed, to provide an elegant and dramatic effect. Some of the patterns are as follows (see Figure 6.6):

Copper: Hammered finish, bright
    Geometric with embossed figures
    Burnished swirls
Pewter: Pebbly textured aluminum, embossd and darkened
Copper: Abstract pattern embossed to highly molten copper splashes
Aluminum: Embossed shiny hammered finish, fine texture
Copper: Abstract design based on Greek fret
Copper: Hammered and partially darkened
Copper: Geometric; larger in scale, embossed to give effect of Oriental calligraphy
Copper: Dark textured abstract
Anodized aluminum: Brushed finish

Stone

Because of its beautiful color and texture, stone is often used in interior work. Its weight poses support problems, but they can sometimes be solved by cutting the stone into rather thin sheets and anchoring or cementing them to a wall or partition. This can be done only when the face of each stone is to be relatively flat.

Many kinds of stone are available, along with a variety of colors—whites, yellows, oranges, browns, and grays. The tonal variation of each kind is usually subtle; most people think of a stone wall as being gray or brown. A close visual analysis of such a wall, however, will reveal an unsuspected number of color variations. The color variations of stone must be taken into consideration when one selects colors to be used near it.

Ideally the stone to be used should be collected either from the site of a proposed building or from adjoining areas; however, even if it is present in sufficient quantity, the cost of gathering and cutting such stone is often so great that it is uneconomical to use local stone for interior work. Suppliers of stone can provide a wide variety which may be selected from sample display walls laid in various patterns. (See Plate 14 for a representative list.) Examples are:

Colorado stone—random ashlar pattern
Lava stone—rubble pattern
Georgia crystal white marble—sawed-bed ashlar pattern

FIG 6.6
Designs in metallic laminates

Wilson Art Brand Laminated Plastic, Temple, TX

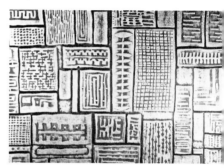

(a)

(b)

Pennsylvania mica—sawed-bed ashlar pattern
Turquoise stone—rubble mosaic pattern
Pine log—rubble mosaic pattern

The following is a list of stones and their color ranges. These are split-face ashlar and rubble veneers, most of which are 4 inches thick; some are heavier, some lighter. In some applications, sawed-bed materials which do not have a concave face can be cut down, usually to a 1-inch thickness, and slotted to receive aluminum anchoring clips. This 1-inch veneer can be applied to any surface material, but cement board or plywood is best. The joints are usually about ½ inch and are pointed with cement. When the joints are filled, of course, it is impossible to tell how thick the veneer is. Also available is a 1-inch veneer termed "Lyte Wall" which can be installed without the aluminum anchoring clips when it is applied to a cement-block back-up. However, if it is applied to frame construction, a galvanized-metal lath and scratch coat must be used.

Stone name	Color	Quarry Location	Availability
Alabama Limestone	Soft buff to silver gray with random black veining	Ala.	U.S.
Alaskan Mix	White, cream to light pink	Alaska	U.S.
Al Cal Mix	Pecan—yellow to beige Moss green pink—green with pink tones Pearl white—cream white Al Cal Mix—white, yellow, beige, green, and pink	Ala.	U.S.
Princeton Ledgrock	Deep brown to purple to deep blue with seam faces of gray, buff, and brown	N.J.	Eastern U.S.
Bluestone	Blue-gray, gray-green, tan, and lilac	N.Y., Pa.	Eastern U.S.
Briar Hill Sandstone	Light gray, buff, light tan, pink variegated, brown, burgundy, and coppertone	Ohio	U.S.
Brownstone	Light to medium brown	Demolished buildings	N.Y. area
Cork Stone	Charcoal brown, medium brown, tan, burnt orange	Texas	U.S.
Bergen Blend Ramapo River Boulders	Tans, gray, brown, rose, and beige	N.J.	Eastern U.S.
Williamsburg Sandstone	Browns, grays, and russet	N.J.	Eastern U.S.
Drift Stone	Gray to brown to red with touch of black	Ariz.	U.S.
Eagle Mountain Onyx	Cream, beige, tan, shades of gold to deep red with a crystal quality	Ariz.	U.S.
Feather River Travertine	Off-white, gray to creamy buff, and light to dark tan	Idaho	U.S.
Featherock	Silver gray, charcoal	Volcanic (Calif.)	U.S.

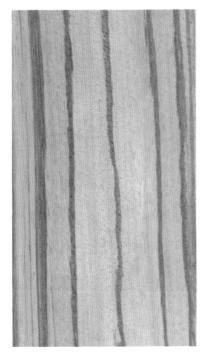

Zebrawood

English brown oak

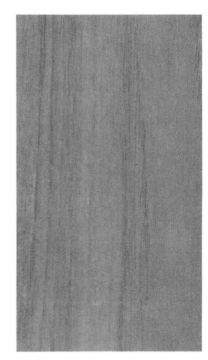

Teak

Kevazingo

Brazilian rosewood

11. Samples of unfinished wood

William L. Marshall, Ltd., New York, NY

Plain-sliced butternut

Quarter-sliced mahogany

Rotary birch

Half-round walnut

Comb-grain oak

Special Figures

Pencil stripe

Fiddleback

Mottled

Blistered

Stumpwood

Feather crotch

Crotch swirl

Birdseye

Crossfire

Ribbon stripe

12. Varied patterns of veneer

*Hardwood Plywood Manufacturers Association, Arlington, VA, and
Fine Hardwoods & American Walnut Association, Chicago, IL*

(a)

13. Uses of plastic laminate
   (a) Study carrel
   (b) Display cases

Wilson Art Brand Laminated Plastic, Temple, TX

(b)

Colorado stone—Random Ashlar Pattern

Lava stone—Rubble Pattern

Pennsylvania mica—Sawed-bed Ashlar Pattern

Georgia crystal white marble—Sawed-bed Ashlar Pattern

Turquoise stone—Rubble Mosaic Pattern

Pine log—Rubble Mosaic Pattern

14. Types of stone

Bergen Bluestone Company, Inc., Paramus, NJ

Stone name	Color	Quarry Location	Availability
Georgia Marble	Crystal white—very white with some gray streaking Pink Etowah—pink with gray and black streaking Creole—white and black swirls Cherokee—white and silver gray with gray streaking Variegated—pale pink with dark gray and black streaking	Ga.	U.S.
Golden Green Range	Green range with subdued browns, tans, reds, and silvers	Pa.	U.S.
Select Green	Green range	Pa.	U.S.
Golden White Onyx	Golden white and white to pale peach	Utah	U.S.
Granite	Grays, tans, pinks, reds, mahogany, variegated blacks, and greens	Various locations	U.S.
Honey Beige	Honey beige, tan, and buff	Ala.	U.S.
Lava Stone	Brownish black	N.Mex.	U.S.
Minnesota Stone	Creams, tans, rusts, browns, and pinks	Minn.	U.S.
Mojave Antique	Cream beige, tan, gold shades to red with a crystal quality	Ariz.	U.S.
Pennsylvania Mica	Silver gray to gold and golden brown	Penn.	U.S.
Pine Log	Ivory, tan, red, buckskin, gray, brown, and buff	Ga.	U.S.
Sable Brown	Rust, deep burgundy and brown-gray with flashes of metallic gold-silver	Ga.	U.S.
Seaford Charcoal	Charcoal gray to metallic silver gray	Ga.	U.S.
Shadow Rock	Tans, reds, light gray, and dark to light brown	Pa.	U.S.
Snow Mountain Crystal	White field with some sections of pale-colored quartz laced with veins of silver and green mica	N.C.	U.S.
Sparkle Gray	Gray-black with heavy mica content	Canada	U.S. & Canada
Sparkle Green	Green with heavy mica content	Canada	U.S. & Canada
Sparkle Red	Deep red with heavy mica content	Canada	U.S. & Canada
Star Black	Black with sparkle	Canada	U.S. & Canada
Tapestry	White with heavy gray-black and golden-bronze stripe veining	Ga.	U.S.
Tennessee Stone	Pink, tan, buff, and variegated	Tenn.	U.S.
Utah Turquoise	Pale green to turquoise	Utah	U.S.
Watauga Silver Green	Silver green	N.C.	U.S.
Western Brownstone	Brown ranges	Ohio	U.S.
White Georgia Chunks	White with gray cloud and veining	Ga.	U.S.
Lyte Wall—1 to 2 in thick			
Cork Stone	Charcoal brown, medium brown, tan, and burnt orange	Texas	U.S.
Featherock	Silver gray, charcoal	Volcanic (Calif.)	U.S.

Stone name	Color	Quarry Location	Availability
Pine Log	Ivory, tan, buckskin, red-gray, brown, and buff	Ga.	U.S.
Rocky Mountain:		Idaho	U.S.
Quartzite	Grays to pinkish tans		
Sunset Gold	Gold and rust		
Sunset Silver	Silver gray to metallic gray		
Sable Brown	Rust, deep burgundy, and brown gray with flashes of metallic gold or silver	Ga.	U.S.
Seaford Charcoal	Charcoal gray to metallic silver gray	Ga.	U.S.

1-inch veneer can be fabricated from the following stones:

Alaskan Marbles	Limestone
Bluestone	Tennessee Stone
Georgia Marbles	Western Brownstone

Courtesy of Bergen Bluestone Co., Inc., 404 Route 17, Paramus, NJ 07652. Local sources, or the Building Stone Institute, 420 Lexington Ave., New York, NY, may be contacted for further information.

Marble

Marble, a crystalline stone, is the result of pressure, heat, and contact with mineral-bearing waters upon limestone. It has a fine, dense texture and takes an excellent polish. Marble varies in color and pattern according to the location in which it is formed. The wide range of colors is caused by the presence in greater or lesser amounts of carbonaceous matter, oxides of iron, graphite, mica, and silica; these ingredients also contribute to the types of grain, or pattern, which are found in the various kinds of marble. Some marble is relatively soft and can be used for interior work only. Hard marble, of course, may be used for interior as well as exterior work. Because of the great expense that the quarrying, cutting, shaping, and finishing of marble entails, marble is today confined to work of major importance. The cost can be brought down by cutting it into thin sheets of, say, ¼ inch and mounting it on interior masonry walls or partitions. Like that of wood, its beauty is in its varying color and pattern. No two pieces are exactly alike, and their variation, as well as the rich appearance that marble produces, provides a highly desired dignity.

Marble can be obtained in several different finishes: polished, honed, sand-rubbed, or abrasive. While smooth finishes tend generally to emphasize color and veining, the rougher finishes tend to subdue veinings or markings. Sawn, tooled, axed, and other finishes are available on special order.

Domestic marble is available from several quarries as listed below.[2] Marble is graded in various categories from "first grade" to grades A, B, and C and is available in many forms from slabs 7 feet long and 6 feet wide (or larger) to rubble chunk veneer. It is advisable to obtain from the source the most reliable data possible as to the suitability of the marble for your purposes before you make a final color decision.

American designers are fortunate in that there are available to them marbles imported from Belgium, Italy, Spain, Mexico, France, Morocco, Canada, Yugoslavia, Portugal, Turkey, Greece, Sweden, Rumania, Iran, England, Switzerland,

[2] *Stone Information Manual, 1976–77*, Building Stone Institute, 420 Lexington Avenue, New York, NY 10017.

Product and Trade Names	Color	Quarry
Georgia Marble		
White Cherokee	White	Georgia Marble Company
Mezzotint	Gray with blue/gray veining	Atlanta, GA 30339
Solar Gray	Gray with blue/gray veining	
Tennessee Cedar		
Cedarchelle	Light beige pink to brown with	Georgia Marble Company
Cedar Tavenelle	tan to brown veining	Atlanta, GA 30339
Rustic Vein		
Mahogany Antique		
Tennex		
Marble		
White Alabama	White and cream to light pink	Moretti-Harrah Marble
Wild and Pink Pitched	and red	Company
Face Veneer		Sylacauga, AL 35150
Madre Cream		
Redstone Rubble		
Champlain Marble		
Champlain Black	From dark gray with mottled	Vermont Marble Company
Grand Isle Fleuri	gray and white markings to	Proctor, VT 05765
Radio Black	deep charcoal gray with small	
	fossils	
Danby Marble		
Danbrook Veined	From white marked with faint	Vermont Marble Company
Highland	clouds of pale tan or gold and	Proctor, VT 05765
Imperial	gray to light pearl gray with	
Mariposa Clouded	subtle darker gray and light	
Mariposa Veined	golden brown markings	
Montclair		
Regal White		
Royal		
Rutland Marble		
Crinkley Vein	From light blue-gray with white	Vermont Marble Company
Mottled White	cloud-like markings to all	Proctor, VT 05765
Vermarco Delft	white; white with shades of	
Light Cloud	light to dark green; and creamy	
Light Vein	white with light to dark green	
Listavena	with striped and clouded	
Pavonazzo	markings	
Statuary		
Striped Brocadillo		
Taconic Green Vein		
Verde Antique Marble		
Vermarco Verde Antique	Deep green background,	Vermont Marble Company
	beautifully veined with various	Proctor, VT 05765
	shades of green and occasional	
	light, almost white markings	

and Peru. A black and white veined marble from France is known as Breche Rencesvalles. Canada contributes a beautiful white marble with a blue cast designated Rideau Blue Fleuri. Lioz Cream is a buff marble from Portugal. A bluish-gray marble referred to as Bardiglietto comes from Italy, as does the green Cipollino Verde Apuano. Red Verona, Red Levanto, and Rosso Alberato also come from Italy, while Rouge Fleuri comes from Rumania. Norwegian Rose is that country's contribution. Mexican onyx is veined with a cream or white background. Morocco sends us Skyros. Blanco P is a beautiful white marble from Italy.

Standard categories of color for marble are as follows:

Black
Blue white
Black and white
Brown
Buff, cream or light
Buff, dark
Gray
Gray, bluish
Green
Red
Rose
Veined (or brecciated)
  Bluish or gray background
  Cream or white background
  Tan or yellowish background
White
Yellow

Limestone is made up of small round grains of carbonate of lime or the remains of skeletons and shells of marine animals. In color it varies from white to gray, cream, or yellowish brown. Sometimes the texture is smooth; sometimes it is pitted by the fossilized remains of sea life.

Travertine is a limestone that has been made porous by running water. It is often used in interior work.

It is wise to examine marble (or any other natural material) before purchasing it. The architect or interior designer should visit the yard of the marble contractor, examine the stock for color and graining, and obtain samples before ordering.

Mirrors

Mirrors in the most primitive form were made of polished bronze in ancient Egypt and ancient Greece. In Greece they were so expensive and highly valued that usually their protective cover was finely decorated. During the Italian Renaissance, Venice, the center of the ornamental glass industry, produced small wall mirrors. Like the hand mirrors of ancient times, they were protected, usually with a wood panel or door, and their frames were also highly decorated. The convex mirror was an invention of the sixteenth century. The modern mirror is a sheet of clear, polished plate glass silvered with a solution of ammonia and silver nitrate. The silvering, which would otherwise decompose in the presence of dampness, is protected with a coat of varnish or shellac and a double coat of lead or of tar paint. Sometimes the silver back is covered by an electrostatically applied layer of copper. The rarity and costliness of mirrors was acknowledged in the past by their magnificent frames of carved wood or pierced metal. A small hand mirror, reflecting only a small image, is practical when it is in use, and ornamental in itself. Wall-hung mirrors, whose function is primarily decorative, are back-coated with dull silver, gold chloride, or lead

FIG. 6.7 Smoky antique mirrors on wall of wet bar, Shapell Studio, Decorator National Association of Mirror Manufacturers, Washington, DC

to give interesting graining, smoky patterns, the appearance of patterned gold metal, or a marbleized effect of, say, black, white, and gold. The appearance of mirrors may also be modified by using tinted plate glass in neutral gray or bronze hues.

Improvements in manufacturing methods have made large mirrors possible. Used in a contemporary interior, large mirrors are designed to reflect not only the image but the color and pattern of areas around it. A small area may be made to appear larger by using expanses of mirror on one wall (see Figure 6.8). Mirrored ceilings, reflecting everything below, create interesting effects. Block mirrors, made of a series of beveled mirror forms, not only reflect things around them but give scale and pattern to a room (see Figure 6.7). A large mirror composed of small units is less expensive and easier to ship and install than a single mirror of the same size.

Ceramic Tile

The word "tile" is all-inclusive. It covers the painted and decorated glazed tiles of ancient Egypt, Assyria, Babylonia, and Persia, the decorative ceramic tile of the Spanish peninsula, the roof tiles of the Orient, the ceramic tiles of Renaissance and post-Renaissance periods in Spain, and the tiles in use today.

Tile, as we know it, is made from a mixture of clays, flint, feldspar, and shales. The various colors, types, and surface finishes of tile are obtained by varying the ingredients and the methods of mixing and firing. Glazed and

FIG. 6.8 *Mirror tiles on wall of dining room Shirley Rogendahl, Designer PPG*
Industries, Pittsburgh, PA

unglazed tile, which may be obtained in many different colors (see Plates 15a and 15b), is used for floors and walls in bathrooms, kitchens, swimming pools, and many other areas where moisture is a problem. It is used decoratively in corridors and lobbies where soil from many hands is a problem, and it is widely used in hospitals and similar buildings where it is necessary to frequently scrub and disinfect floors and walls.

The early tile makers used local clays which were moistened and worked into shape in single pieces. Sometimes color was introduced into the body of the tile, but in some localities a colored glaze was made separately and applied to the tile as ornamentation. Crude baked tiles with painted decorations were made in the Mayan and Aztec civilizations. Blue delft tiles were made in Holland. Early Colonial settlers had tile shipped to America from Europe and faced their fireplaces with picture tiles from England and Holland.

There are two basic methods of manufacturing tile. In the "plastic method," the materials are hand-molded; in the "dust-pressed" method, the excess water is removed and the almost-dry material is pressed into shape by machines. Unglazed tile obtains its colors from the ingredients used—in particular, the kinds of clays and oxides that can be added to the clays.

It was in 1876 that the first serious attempts were made to produce tile in the United States. These were crude, but nevertheless they used a one-fire process in which body and glaze were fused by firing together. Improvements continued to be made in manufacturing processes and are still being made today.

Whereas the colors of tile used to be determined by local clays and materials, today raw materials are brought to the tile manufacturer from many different areas: flour-like talc from upper New York State, pyrophyllite from North Carolina and Newfoundland, china clay from Florida, flint from West Virginia, and coloring substances from other distant places. One of the larger tile manufacturers prepares the materials by blending them with water, which is then removed, together with foreign matter; the resultant finely powdered clay is then pressed into shape under great pressure. The glazed coating is automatically sprayed on in liquid form, its thickness regulated to 0.001 inch. In the firing process, the tile is very slowly passed through large kilns under intense heat. Because of the slight differences in the various materials that are used, it often happens that tiles of the same type will vary somewhat in color. The colors for each shipment are carefully selected for color consistency.

Tiles made by various companies differ. It is interesting to note that for the benefit of the trade, as well as that of the consumer, the Tile Council of America, Inc. started a cooperative effort by members, nonmembers, and various segments of the ceramic tile industry to revise the existing specifications for the manufacture and use of ceramic tile. This was printed by the Tile Council of America, Inc. and entitled "Recommended Standard Specifications for Ceramic Tile" (TCA 137.1-1976, for use and reference after December 31, 1975). This booklet provides information and definitions regarding the various types, sizes, physical properties, and grading procedures for ceramic tile in the United States. While tile manufacturers are not obliged to adhere to these standards, those who do are encouraged to indicate such conformance on tags and labels as well as in their advertising.

For purposes of grade marking and certification, and for the ultimate protection of the consumer, the Recommended Standard Specifications define the following:

> *Standard Grade*—Ceramic tiles that meet the requirements of these specifications.
> *Second Grade*—Ceramic tiles that meet all of the requirements of these specifications except that inspection for facial defects is conducted at a distance of 10 feet instead of 3 feet.

Test procedures are as outlined by the specifications of the American Society for Testing Materials, and they cover such technical items as water absorption, bulk density, apparent porosity, crazing resistance, bond strength, warpage, facial dimensions and thickness, relative resistance to wear, wedging, small color differences, and breaking strength.

The different kinds of tile may be described as follows:

Tile A ceramic surfacing unit, usually relatively thin in relation to facial area, made from clay or a mixture of clay and other ceramic materials, called the body of the tile, having either a glazed or unglazed face and fired above red heat in the course of manufacture to a temperature sufficiently high to produce specific properties and characteristics.

Ceramic mosaic tile Tile formed by either the dust-pressed or plastic method, usually ¼ to ⅜ inch thick and having a facial area of less than 6 square inches. Ceramic mosaic tiles may be of either porcelain or natural clay composition, and they may be either plain or with an abrasive mixture throughout.

Conductive tile Tile made from special body composition or by methods that result in specific properties of electrical conductivity while retaining other normal physical properties of tile.

Glazed tile Tile with a fused impervious facial finish composed of ceramic materials, fused to the body of the tile, which may be nonvitreous, semivitreous, vitreous, or impervious.

Impervious tile Tile with water absorption of 0.5 percent or less.

Mounted tile Tile assembled into units or sheets bonded by suitable material to facilitate handling. Tile may be back-mounted or face-mounted. Back-mounted tile has perforated paper, fiber mesh, resin, or other suitable bonding material permanently attached to the backs and/or edges of the tile so that a portion of the back surface of each tile is exposed to the bond coat. Face-mounted tile has paper applied to the faces of the tile, usually by water-soluble adhesive so that it can be easily removed prior to grouting of the joints.

Natural clay tile A ceramic mosaic tile or a paver tile made by either the dust-pressed or the plastic method from clays that produce a dense body having a distinctive, slightly textured appearance.

Nonvitreous tile Tile with water absorption of more than 7 percent.

Paver tile Unglazed porcelain or natural clay tile formed by the dust-pressed method and similar to ceramic mosaic tile in composition and physical properties, but relatively thicker, with 6 square inches or more of facial area.

Porcelain tile A ceramic mosaic tile or paver tile that is generally made by the dust-pressed method of a composition resulting in a tile that is dense, impervious, fine-grained, and smooth, with a sharply formed face.

Pregrouted (or edgebonded) tile A surfacing unit consisting of an assembly of ceramic tiles bonded together at their edges by a material, generally elastomeric, which seals the joints completely. Such material (grout) may fill the joint completely or partially, and may cover all, a portion, or none of the face surfaces of the tiles in the sheets. The perimeter of these factory-pregrouted sheets may include the entire joint or part of the joint between the sheets, or none at all. The term "edgebonded tile" is sometimes used to designate a particular type of pregrouted tile sheet having the front and back surfaces completely exposed.

Quarry tile   Unglazed tile, usually 6 square inches or more in surface area and ½ to ¾ inch thick, made by the extrusion process from natural clay or shale.

Self-spacing tile   Tile with lugs, spacers, or protuberances on the sides which automatically space the tile for grout joints.

Semivitreous tile   Tile with water absorption of more than 3 percent but not more than 7 percent.

Slip-resistant tile   Tile having greater slip-resistant characteristics due to an abrasic admixture, abrasive particles in the surface, or grooves or patterns in the surface.

Special-purpose tile   Tile, either glazed or unglazed, made in accordance with special physical design or appearance characteristics such as size, thickness, shape, color, or decoration; keys or lugs on backs or sides; pregrouted assemblies or sheets; special resistance to staining, frost, alkalies, acids, thermal shock, physical impact, or high coefficient of friction.

Trim units   Units of various shapes consisting of such items as bases, caps, corners, moldings, angles, etc., which are necessary to achieve an installation of the desired sanitary and/or architectural design.

Unglazed tile   A hard, dense tile of uniform composition throughout, deriving color and texture from the materials of which the body is made.

Vitreous tile   Tile with water absorption of more than 0.5 percent but not more than 3 percent.

Wall tile   A glazed tile that has a body suitable for interior use, is usually nonvitreous, and is not required or expected to withstand excessive impact or to be subject to freezing and thawing conditions.

The various tile manufacturers make available to architects and interior designers charts and samples of the colors of the tile they manufacture. Listed here is the line of one domestic producer, American Olean Tile Company; this consists of the firm's Bright and Matte tile for walls, counters, and exteriors (the asterisks signify matte glazes):

*Gloss Black	*Suntan	*Fern Green
*Smoke Gray	Honeysuckle	*Sage Gray
*Dawn Gray	*Pink Blush	*Bayberry
Antique	*Hydrangea	Salt & Pepper
*Brite White	Avocado	*Spruce
Gardenia	Autumn Gold	Robin's Egg
*Nutmeg	*Daffodil	Aqua Mist
*Parchment	Buttercup	Cornflower
Vellum	*Jonquil	Lobelia
Buckwheat	*Cream	Pastel Blue
Gold Mist	Sylvan Green	Flax Blue
Sandalwood	Spring Green	Orchid

*FIG. 6.9 Bath using Wenczel Antigua CrystaLace and color-coordinated square tile
Tile Council of America, Princeton, NJ*

Accent colors for the foregoing tiles, intended for random decorative use, are available in a high glaze in the following colors:

Cherry Red	Meadow Green
Vermilion	Brite Blue
Tangerine	Regal Blue
Lemon Yellow	Violet

The Bright and Matte tiles are available in these sizes:
$4\frac{1}{4} \times 4\frac{1}{4}$ in, $6 \times 4\frac{1}{4}$ in, 6×6 in, and $8\frac{1}{2} \times 4\frac{1}{4}$ in
Tile gems[3]: $1\frac{3}{8} \times 1\frac{3}{8}$ in

Frostproof tile body can be obtained in $4\frac{1}{4} \times 4\frac{1}{4}$ inch size. Tile for interior use is 5/16 inch thick, while frostproof tile is 11/32 inch thick. Trim units, bathroom fixtures, and other special items for specific installations are available.

Other patterns of decorative tile such as Primitive, Terra Vitra, Sculptured, Tuscany, Crystalline, and Scored are available in a variety of colors, sizes, and shapes. Patterned tiles with high and low reliefs provide yet another variation of this versatile decorative material.

Floor tile, which can also be used for walls and counters, includes patterns such as Caribbean, Pomona Glazed Tile, and PomonaStone Caribbean is available in the 3×6 inch size; Pomona Glazed Tile comes in the $4\frac{1}{4} \times 4\frac{1}{4}$ and 6×6 inch sizes, while PomonaStone is available in 6×6 and 9×9 inches.

Ceramic mosaics, termed Clearline and Texline by American Olean, have a fine-grained tile body with the color throughout the tile. They are impervious, with less than 0.5 percent absorption, stainproof, dentproof, and frostproof. As they are suitable for interior and exterior floors, walls in all types of buildings, and countertops, they form an extremely flexible surfacing for both indoor and outdoor applications. With twenty-eight colors available in the Clearline

[3] Registered Trademark, American Olean Tile Co.

group and sixteen in the Texline, flecked with white, there is a wide choice of color. Sizes range from 2 × 2 inches to 2 × 1 and 1 × 1 inch. Special slip-resistant abrasive is available in certain colors. Clearline or Texline tiles are also available in thirty-two stock patterns combining several colors and sizes to provide yet another variation for consideration.

Quarry tile is manufactured from carefully graded shale and fire clays extruded to produce a strong, hard body which is noted for its durability and easy maintenance (see Plate 40). Seven earth-tone colors such as Ember Flash, Canyon Red, Sand Flash, Umber, Fawn Gray, Sahara, and Golden Glow are available. They can be obtained in a number of sizes and shapes:

Squares: 6 × 6, 4 × 4, 2¾ × 2¾, and 8 × 8 in
Rectangles: 2¾ × 6 and 3⅞ × 8 in
Hexagon: 6, 8, and 8-in elongated hexagon
Valencia: 8 × 6 and 10 × 8 in

A variation of quarry tile is "Tahoe," which has an undulating texture compressed into the surface of the tile. It can be used for interior and exterior walls, light- and moderate-usage residential floors and countertops. While it is available in seven glazes such as Glacier, Azure, Nugget, Burnt Copper, Ponderosa, Bark, and Cordova, there are shade variations within each tile and from tile to tile which impart a special interest. Tahoe comes in 3⅞ × 8 and 8-inch hexagon shapes, 8 × 6 and 10 × 8 inch valencia shape, and the 8-inch elongated hexagon.

As you can see from the foregoing, there is a wide variety of colors, shapes, and patterns in ceramic tile. There are also decorated tiles with designs of sea life, seashells, vegetables, decanters, grain, animals, and geometric forms.

Other variations include such tiles as "Triton," by Briare Company, which is made of hardened impervious glass and has a curved diabolo shape 1⅝ inches long. It is available in sable, rose, perle, ecaille (rust), algue (olive green), varech (slate blue), ombrine (soft brown), blue marine (dark blue), onde (medium blue), and dune (a soft light tan).

The "Gemmes" pattern of Briare tile is a 1-inch hexagonal in colors such as cymophane (pale gold), heliotrope (olive green), onyx, opale (white), chrysocole (bright blue), azurite (sky blue), pierre de soleil (red-orange), and rhodonite (pink).

Handcrafted tiles are available in various colors and patterns, and, like all handcrafted materials, they are artistically handsome because of their imperfections.

Since tile is available in so many different colors and shapes, it is possible for the architect or interior designer to use the available "alphabet" in many ways (see Plates 15a and 15b). Anyone can use a single-colored tile, but it takes a skilled and practiced professional to combine tile colors and sizes to accentuate the good points of architectural spaces. If such a space is very high, horizontal patterns will be called for, but if the space has a low ceiling, vertical stripes or other patterns will help to "raise" it. In rooms with a moderately large floor surface, suggested standard patterns in various color combinations are offered by manufacturers. The choice of floor and wall tiles will depend upon the size of the room, the directional effect that the architect or designer wishes to obtain, and, of course, the colors that are required.

Murals can also be created, and the colors of the tiles must be selected by the principles described in Chapter 1 on color theory. Colors must be integrated with other colors in the area; the mural designer will usually cooperate with the architect and designer in achieving the desired effect.

FLOORING

Carpets and Rugs

Carpets seem to have originated in the Orient, and traders probably introduced them to Europe. They were so highly esteemed that they were often hung as wall decorations. Carpet designs varied according to the locality in which they were made. It has been suggested that patterns containing flowers, trees, and animals[4] reflected the importance of these items to Oriental people, who enjoyed surrounding themselves with these objects.

While in some places animals were used in the design, in others human figures were occasionally portrayed. But basically one finds symbols which are expressions of the spiritual world.[5] In addition to symbolism in design, a complete and elaborate color symbolism was used. One's rank and status partially determined the design of one's carpet: A carpet made for a prince was different from one made for a person of lesser importance. Colors varied from country to country and from tribe to tribe. Green might be the sacred color of Muhammad and, therefore, be used for prayers. In another country, blue might symbolize power. Many plants were symbolically important. One finds that the various seasons were represented by specific flowers, and the tree of life seems to have been present in almost every Oriental carpet. Animals and insects were important too in the symbolic scheme of things. The butterfly signified longevity; the scarab, royal power in India. Geometrical figures of significance going back thousands of years include the triangle, the meander pattern, and the Buddhist arc. Regardless of the design elements, however, a central motif is a part of almost every Oriental rug. Here people could sit or recline and survey the beauties of the design which surrounded them.

One of the characteristics of the genuine Oriental rug is its thinness. When the makers of rugs in Europe and the United States tried to imitate Oriental rugs, they added a backing to which the surface pile was woven.

Today, in the age of the power loom, rugs (which are used individually) and carpets (which can be sewn together) are manufactured in three different ways: woven, knitted, or tufted.

Woven carpet The surface pile and backing of woven carpet are interwoven at the same time, creating a single fabric. Due to the interweaving, which locks all the yarns together in the single-woven fabric, the pile yarns cannot be pulled out. Some carpet weaves presently available are velvet, Wilton, and Axminster. Velvet is best suited for solid-color carpet; however, tweeds, stripes, and salt-

---

[4] *Ciba Review*, Vols. 1–24, September 1937–August 1939, p. 517.

[5] Ibid., p. 525.

and-pepper effects can be produced on velvet looms. The usual velvet is a solid-color carpet with smooth surface and even pile. Sometimes the pile is cut to produce a plushlike surface (see Figure 6.10a). It may also be had in loop pile or twist.

Wilton weave comes in almost unlimited numbers of textures and sculptured effects, as well as patterns. The pile is sometimes cut, sometimes left uncut; a combination of cut and uncut may also be obtained. In multicolor Wiltons, one color may be seen on the surface pile, while other colors are hidden in the body of the carpet. Embossed and sculptured effects are also made by the Wilton looms and uncut pile can be combined with cut pile for the top level, with loops at other levels. Another variation is to have some pile yarn straight and others twisted (see Figure 6.10b).

In the Axminster weave, which is similar in appearance to handweaving, we find a complete flexibility in the use of color. In this method each tuft is inserted separately, and while solid-color carpets can be made this way, Axminster weave is nearly always used for multicolored-pattern carpets such as Orientals or for modern and geometric designs (see Figure 6.10c).

Tufted carpet In the tufted process, which was only recently perfected, the tufts are attached to a previously made backing; this differs from the methods described above, in which the backing and pile are integral. The tufts are held in place by a heavy coating of latex applied to the backing, which is usually cotton, jute, or kraft cord. By the use of this method, a wide variety of textures is possible. For example, the tufted pile can be made in several levels; it can be cut or uncut; and carved or striated effects can be obtained. The pile can be looped or plush. Tufted carpets are made in multicolor patterns with an increasing number of textural effects and refinements (see Figure 6.10d).

While the production of patterned carpet by hand or even jacquard loom is a time-consuming process, new techniques in dyeing while the carpet is being manufactured have been perfected. Although highly sophisticated equipment is required, the results are so efficient and versatile that contemporary patterned carpeting is widely available.

Knitted carpet The knitting process loops together the pile yarn, backing yarn, and stitching yarn with three sets of needles in a manner similar to knitting. Finally a coat of latex is applied on the back. Because a single-pile yarn is used for the knitting process, these carpets are usually tweeds or solid colors, and they are made with cut or uncut loops either in single level or multilevel. Cut pile can be obtained by modifying the machines.

Selecting the color When selecting the color of a carpet, one must realize that it will bring a great deal of color into an area and that, generally speaking, the carpet color should be darker than the wall color because it will show less soil and will have a more comfortable reflectance value. A carpet's texture makes it appear darker than a smooth surface of the same color; therefore a carpet will seem to be darker than the color of its yarn. In most cases, contrasting schemes obtained by making the carpet a complement of the wall color produce too sharp an effect, and unless other factors enter into the decision, the walls and carpet should be kept in the same color family. For instance, a red carpet will be very effective in a room with pale pink walls, or a blue-green carpet can be used in a room where the draperies are blue and the chairs are green.

FIG. 6.10 Carpet construction
(a) Velvet weave
(b) Wilton weave
(c) Axminster weave
(d) Tufted carpet

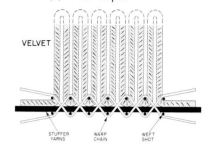

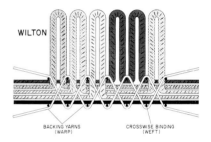

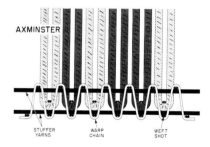

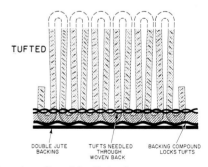

American Carpet Institute, Inc.
(integrated with Carpet Cushion
Council, Dalton, GA)

On the other hand, a creamy white carpet can be effectively used as a foil for medium green walls and white and green furniture and accessories (see Plate 25).

As might be expected, the most unusual colors are available in higher-priced lines, and less expensive carpets are offered in a limited number of colors. (If carpets were available in every color and shade, a carpet store's range of selections would still be limited, because it would be able to stock only so many of them.) The limited range of available carpet colors sometimes makes it impossible for experienced designers to find the more subtle colors they prefer to use, and at that point they turn to custom carpet. However, the carpet market is still extremely flexible, and stock carpet is available to solve the majority of problems satisfactorily. In addition to color, the end use should be considered when selecting carpeting, and usually the manufacturer's literature or label will be a guide. Such qualities as durability, sound absorption, and hygienic properties should be considered. Natural fibers such as wool and cotton have many desirable qualities, as do the artificial fibers, and thorough research is required to make a knowledgeable judgment as to the right carpet for the problem at hand.

The color lines in a typical carpet salesroom vary according to material and manufacture. Color lines might include the following:

Wool

(As wool is yellowish in color, no very bright white, pale pink, or pale yellow carpet can be made of it.)

Yellow white	Pumpkin	Avocado
Pale gray	Terra-cotta	Blue green
Gray green	Beige	Scarlet
Light blue	Light yellow	Deep red
Pale gray blue	Lemon yellow	Taupe
Orange	Yellow green	Brown

Both solid colors and mixtures would be available in various weaves.

Nylon

Red	Fairway green	Zephyr blue
Slate	Hot pepper	Autumn air
Antique brass	Seascape	New gold
Marigold	Bronze gold	Blue green
Tweed:	Pine green	Russet
Bittersweet	Stone	Cardinal
Ripe Avocado	Mahogany	

Nylon has a luster, and colors are vibrant.

Propylene and other special synthetics

Peacock blue	Mesa orange	Golden grain
Cherry red	Gothic gold	Blue green
Oxford gray	Nutmeg	Sapphire
Driftwood	Valley green	
Island sand	Tudor gray	

Acrylic

Neutrals:	Oatmeal	Pebble
Adobe	Granite	Mink
Dove	Sandlewood	Loam

| Slate | Oak | Charglow |
| Espresso | Charblue | |

Colors:

Brilliant orange	Gray gold	Green
Brilliant red	Sky blue	Avocado
Orange red	Medium blue	Taupe
Gold	Dark blue	

Acrylic fiber has a wool-like appearance.

Cotton carpets can be manufactured in practically any color or combination of colors, and usually there is a wide range to choose from.

Various blends of wool and nylon, Acrilan acrylic and modacrylic, and other synthetics are on the market in an assortment of colors to answer a great many requirements.

Many suppliers will dye carpets to special order, and while this practice is common, it should not be entered into lightly because of the relatively high cost. It takes an experienced eye to approve small swatches of yarn color even to prepare a "strike-off," and the strike-off is but an indication of what the installation will actually look like.

Area rugs, unlike carpet, do not cover the entire floor. They may be plain or patterned (see Plates 16a and 16b), and virtually any rug is suitable for any room if its color has been given proper consideration when planning the entire color scheme. Whereas broadloom carpet laid wall to wall is usually considered a background, rugs very often act as a focal point. Interestingly enough, most rugs that are sold by the better suppliers are monochromatic. In previous times, such as the age of Louis XIV, rugs were sold only to the nobility, but the demand for them became so great that they were soon sold to all who could pay for them in order to help support the extravagances of the court.

With a rich background of design and color at hand, the modern rug designer often styles a contemporary version of Savonnerie or Aubusson or other traditional styles. Some of these are developed in as many as six color combinations. Using their own colors, today's designers make their rugs adaptable to contemporary usage. They are often designed to order and are usually created as follows:

1. The architect or interior designer selects a pattern.

2. The colors are selected in accordance with the color scheme. (Earth colors are often used in contemporary rugs.)

3. The manufacturer makes a full-scale rendering showing the relationship of colors in the pattern.

4. The client and designer are shown the rendering, and they select the yarns.

5. A strike-off 2 feet square is made by the manufacturer.

6. When the strike-off is approved, all of the above items are sent to the factory and the rug is completed.

Modern rugs have the beauty of tapestries, and entire color schemes can be built around one. Frequently their color and pattern are an integral part of the total design of the area.

Both manufacturer and client are responsible for tastes in colors. It is interesting that certain shades seem to be perennially popular—for example, french putty, which is neutral and beautiful; a bright cherry red (especially lovely on stairways); and a mousy taupe color. A beautifully proportioned and designed neutral rug of warm gray or gray brown, with a small amount of cerulean blue, never goes out of style.

Resilient flooring

Tiles Early experiments in producing a practical, economical, and decorative floor covering for concrete floors were primitive and discouraging, but they led the way to developments which, about 1922, produced heartening results. A mastic, made of a resinous binder and some asbestos, developed into a heavy-duty floor tile that could be used on concrete flooring, both on or below grade.

By 1926–1927 marbleizing was developed, together with improved formulas and pigments. Lighter colors were manufactured, and the popularity of asphalt tile increased. Vinyl asbestos tile, combining these two durable raw materials, evolved from asphalt tile about 1939. Due to World War II shortages, it was not available to the public until 1948, when 9- by 9- by ⅛-inch tiles were

FIG. 6.11 Coordinated flooring and wallpaper, Armstrong Decoresq Collection
Armstrong Cork Company, Lancaster, PA

produced for commercial use. By 1953 it was available for residential use in 1/16-inch gauge. Rubber and vinyl tile made their appearance on the market at about the same time.

Developments in manufacture since then have progressed from surface decoration to semitranslucent chips embedded in the ground and embossed patterns; and more sophisticated printing techniques provided new degrees of subtle coloration. Today many designs extend throughout the thickness of the tile. Such advantages as durability against soil and wear, economy, easy installation, and simple maintenance make resilient floor tiles a colorful and practical tool for the architect and interior designer.

Sheet Another type of resilient floor is sheet vinyl, which had its origins in oilcloth (a woven fabric coated with oil or paint and then varnished and rubbed smooth). "Linoleum" appeared in the early twentieth century, but it was not until a way was found to manufacture an enameled felt base that it was possible to reduce the cost of manufacture to make it available to a broader market. Even though design possibilities were limited and it could not be used below grade, it was a popular floor covering. With the advent of vinyl resin and inorganic fillers, as well as rotogravure-printed designs, sheet vinyl was improved in color and durability, and manufacturing techniques kept the cost of the product economical. Improvements in the backing were developed, including a foam inter-layer to produce cushioned varieties. The addition of a high-gloss surface on some patterns resulted in still easier maintenance.[6]

Today a resilient floor can be installed in virtually any area. Most varieties are sheet vinyl, vinyl asbestos tile, or vinyl tile, although asphalt tile is also available through some manufacturers. Inspiration for patterns for resilient flooring is taken from natural materials or other relatively expensive floor coverings, the cost of which would be prohibitive for many installations. From the many designs and types available, there is a wide variety of solutions to almost any problem. A thorough study of the items available is necessary to produce the best results. In addition to color, one should consider the manufacturer's recommended-usage data on such items as durability, ease of maintenance, fire and burn resistance, resilience, and in-room quietness. If the visible floor area is a major part of the room, light reflectance is important, and this can also be checked with the supplier for accurate information.

Sheet vinyl *(vinyl resins with asbestos fiber back)* Sheet vinyl is usually available in rolls 6 feet wide, but some are 12 feet wide. Various patterns are offered by the different manufacturers in smooth finish, textured, cushioned, and no-wax (see Figure 6.11). Here are some of the patterns and colors offered by Armstrong Cork Company:

VINYL CORLON FLOORING

> *Random Texture:* Gold, beige, green, white, russet
> *Grand Central:* White, beige, gray-beige
> *Houndstooth Check:* White, beige, gold, orange, green
> *Coronelle:* Bricktone—natural red, white
> *Arlmont:* Spanish tile—Coruna brown, Granada gold, burnt orange
> *San Marco:* Stone paving—white, bayberry, red
> *Flagstone:* Rutland green

[6] Technical Manual, 2d ed., 1976; GAF Corporation, Building Materials Group, Floor Products, New York, NY 10020.

*FIG. 6.12   Dining room using Gafstar Deluxe sheet vinyl, Dutch Royale pattern
GAF Corporation, Floor Products, New York, NY*

American Favorite: Stone paving—gold, beige, red
Colony Bay: Spanish tile—brown, white, gold, red
Montina: Pebble chips—sand beige, teak black
Brigantine: Char brown, zinnia, nutmeg, burnt ochre, beige-white, gold, orange, white, cork, brown
Palestra: Pebble chips—frost white, bayberry, gold, beige, tan, brown, white

CUSHIONED VINYL FLOORING

Villa Cortez: Spanish tile—gold, orange, green, beige
Santa Flora: Spanish tile—white w/gray, yellow w/white, green w/white, blue w/white
Country Flower: White w/tan, yellow w/rust, ochre w/black, terra-cotta w/ beige, blue w/tan
Viacci: White w/gray, green w/white, terra-cotta in three shades, brown w/ rust and beige

CUSHIONED ROTOVINYL (*no-wax finish*)

Variety of patterns in colors such as white, green/gold, orange/gold, beige, blue, yellow, butterscotch, green, brown, terra-cotta

MULTI-LAYER VINYL

Variety of patterns in colors such as glo-white, brown, red, beige

NO-WAX VINYL

Various patterns in floral, brick, tile, plaid, etc., in colors such as yellow, orange, gold, coral, terra-cotta, blue/white, honey, white, beige, red/gold, blue/gold, white/gold, green, orange, tan, bisque

Resilient Tile   The Resilient Tile Institute each year publishes a Color Comparison Chart for Vinyl Asbestos Tile, as well as tile specifications, information on adhesives, and cleaner and wax specifications. The chart also contains installation specifications and maintenance recommendations. In the Color Comparison Chart, standard-size 12- by 12- by ⅛-inch-thick tiles as manufactured by Amtico, Armstrong, Azrock, Flintkote, GAF, and Kentile are compared. Each firm's pattern is indicated, along with their pattern numbers, in the following color categories:

Chip Patterns—Vinyl asbestos tile—12 × 12 × ⅛ in (3/32-in thickness available in some cases)

Black	Green/olive
Brown or taupe	Gray, gray-beige
Tan or cedar	White-black
Beige	White-other
Cream/sand/gold	Blue
Green	Red/orange

Marble Patterns—Vinyl asbestos tile—12 × 12 × ⅛ in (3/32-in thickness available in some cases)

Black with white marbleizing
Red with white or yellow marbleizing
Beige-gray with white or tan marbleizing
Cream/sand/yellow with white, tan, or other marbleizing
Green with white or other marbleizing
White with black marbleizing
White with varied marbleizing
Blue with white and blue marbleizing

Comparisons are given for special marble patterns, embossed travertine patterns, plain colors, polished marble chip patterns, and textured stone patterns, but not all manufacturers produce all items.

The following is a comparison of colors and patterns in vinyl composition tiles (12- by 12- by ⅛-inch) offered by three manufacturers:[7]

ARMSTRONG'S EXCELON Travertex

Briar Tan: Tan w/brown flecks
Frost White: Blue white with black and gray flecks
Cream White: Cream white with brown flecks
Harvest Ivory: Beige with brown flecks
Nougat Beige: Deep beige with brown flecks

AMTICO'S TRAVATILE (ALSO AVAILABLE IN 3/32-INCH)

White and Beige: Creamy beige ground with chocolate veining
Eggshell: Beige ground with deep beige veining

KENTILE'S AVANTI (ALSO IN 1/16-AND 3/32-INCH)

Parma Beige: Gray beige ground with brown and white flecks
Alpine White: Greenish white with beige and white grain
Venetian Suede: Pale gray with brown and white grain
Bergamo Gray: Gray with white and dark gray grain
Salerno Cream: Cream ground with cream and white grain

[7] 1976 Color Comparison Charts, Resilient Tile Institute, 26 Washington St., East Orange, NJ 07017.

Armstrong has two patterns in 12 by 12 by ⅛-inch or 3/32-inch-gauge vinyl asbestos tile as follows:

MARBLEIZED PATTERN

Cottage Tan	Tent Olive
Shelter White	Casa Orange
Fortress White	Teahouse Blue
Pagoda Red	Temple Orange
Manor Green	Mansion Gold
Tower Gold	Castle Greige
Palace Beige	Cathedral Gold

NON-DIRECTIONAL GRAINING

Fleece White	Mellow Sand
Char Brown	Medium Cork
Bayberry White	Olive
Sandrift White	

In through-grained vinyl composition tiles, Armstrong has marbleized patterns as indicated above and grained patterns called "Embossed Classic Travertine" in white and beige. An embossed grain pattern is also available in white bayberry, fawn white, and Iroquois tan.

Feature strips for custom floor design, 1 by 24 inches, and solid colors for accent are available in Black, Chocolate II, Neutral II, Yellow II, Orange II, White I, Red I, Celery I, Gold I, and Blue II.

Vinyl cove base is available in 2½- and 4-inch heights, .080-inch gauge, in embossed colors of medium walnut, teak, and brown stone, and in plain colors of black, burnt umber, walnut, beige, white, bone white and buff.

The reaction of resilient floors to fire or heat is often important, and most manufacturers can provide specific information about their product. Kentile offers a solid vinyl tile, 18 by 18 by ⅛ inches, which, they say, does not support combustion. It is called Casa Vista, a patterned clay tile which is available in Desert Frost, Pueblo Clay, Palomino, and Canyon Sunset. Special sizes can also be obtained on special order.

Custom design enables the architect or interior designer to balance color and scale, as well as to define areas. In Plate 18a, beige defines the entire area and leads to the elevator door. The russet color is used not only as accent but to define the seating area and the information counter. In Plate 18b, white is used as an accent for the gray-beige of the major floor area. One needs only imagination—and an adequate budget.

Cork

A comfortable and beautiful floor can be obtained by the use of cork tile. Since cork is a natural material and is ground and mixed with a binder before it is pressed into shape, a fair amount of color variation can be expected. These colors will range from a medium gray orange to a gray brown. Because of the process of manufacture, it is also possible to obtain a great many different effects. For instance, a pattern may contain alternate strips of light, finely ground cork and darker, coarser cork. As with wood, the colors in which cork is available are relatively neutral; almost any color may be used with it. Furthermore, the cork enhances the colors. In addition to its use as a flooring material, cork may be used as a finish for walls; it is available in sheets for wall application.

Terrazzo

Terrazzo, a composite material, is usually poured in place but may be precast. It is generally used for walls or floors when beauty and strength are desired. Terrazzo is made from chips of marble, onyx, or other rock capable of being ground to various sizes from 0 (about 1/16 inch) to 8 (about 1 inch). Various sizes and kinds of chips are skillfully combined, and a wide range of patterns is available. The National Terrazzo and Mosaic Association, Inc., 716 Church St., Alexandria, VA 22314, publishes a book of plates showing combinations of chips and colors of patterns. Standard plates are those patterns frequently used and readily available. The combinations have been formulated by expert color consultants after extensive research into architectural and interior design requirements. If custom designs are desired, they should be carefully studied with a reliable terrazzo contractor.

The color categories of the chips used in the formulation of terrazzo are as follows:

White	Rose
Black	Gray (blue)
Dark green	Brown
Light green	Buff-tan
Dark red	Cream
Light red	Yellow
Pink	

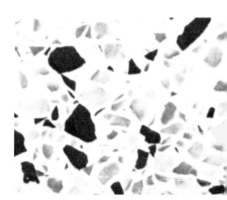

Terrazzo chips are sprinkled (or embedded) in a binder that can be cementitious, chemical, or a combination of both. After the terrazzo is poured, it is cured, ground, and polished, or otherwise finished to a uniformly textured surface. Most standard terrazzo uses chips in various combinations of No. 1 and No. 2 chips. Venetian terrazzo is made from larger chips. Palladiano terrazzo utilizes thin random-fractured slabs of marble, sometimes with standard terrazzo joints between each slab. Rustic terrazzo is uniformly textured, and the matrix is depressed to expose the chips.

Matrices such as white portland cement, gray cement, or tinted cement are used, as are chemical compounds such as epoxy resin, polyester resin, polyacrylate, or eatex. Conductive matrix is available where required to conduct electricity with regulated resistance. Terrazzo can be installed in various thicknesses and by different methods to suit specific requirements. Divider strips are available in aluminum, white alloy of zinc, brass, or plastic. When working on a terrazzo installation, the designer should obtain a physical sample of the actual terrazzo pattern from the contractor for approval before the job is begun.

Remember that in selected varicolored terrazzo floors, the finished appearance (what one sees when the material has been completely installed) is an average of all the colors used. A description of the color of the chips in a random selection of terrazzo plates follows:

*FIG. 6.13   Terrazzo samples
The National
Terrazzo and
Mosaic
Association, Inc.,
Arlington, VA*

Plate No.	Cement	Chips
S-102	Gray cement	75% white chips, 15% dark green, 10% light green
S-103	White cement	50% white, 50% cream
S-104	White cement	60% white, 20% dark red, 20% pink
S-106	White cement	50% white, 30% blue, 20% gray
S-108	White cement	80% blue, 20% black
S-111	White cement	80% blue, 20% light green
S-112	Gray with 1 lb. black pigment	60% black, 40% blue
S-113	50% white, 50% gray cement	70% black, 30% cream
S-119	White cement	60% brown, 30% buff/tan, 10% dark cream
S-129	White cement	70% rose, 30% cream
S-132	White cement	100% rose
S-133	Gray with ½ lb. yellow pigment	50% yellow, 30% cream, 20% dark cream
S-135	Gray cement	50% dark red veined, 30% brown, 20% dark red solid
S-139	Gray cement	80% dark red, 10% yellow, 10% cream
S-140	White cement	80% light green, 20% dark green
S-141	White cement	80% light green, 20% white
S-148	Gray cement	60% light red, 40% cream
S-150	Gray with ½ lb. black pigment	100% dark red
S-151	Gray cement	70% light red, 20% gray, 10% black
S-154	White with ½ lb. black pigment ½ lb. green pigment ½ lb. yellow pigment	60% dark green, 40% light green
S-176	Gray with ¼ lb. turquoise pigment and ¼ lb. black pigment	40% gray, 50% light green, 10% dark green
S-181	Chemical red cement	40% light red #1, 20% fines, 40% black #1
Venetian		
V-101	50% white cement 50% gray cement	100% light green venetian
V-102	Gray with ½ lb. black pigment and 1 lb. green pigment	60% light green venetian, 40% dark green venetian
Rustic Terrazzo		
R-108	Gray with ¾ lb. black pigment	60% black #2, 40% blue #2

Wood Flooring

The beauty of wood flooring is not only in the wood that may be used, but also in the variation of color and pattern which the natural product supplies. Custom finishes on the job can range from clear to stained to provide the most satisfactory solution to the problem.

There are four basic types of wood flooring: strip, plank, parquet, and fabricated wood blocks. Wood floors may be of walnut, beech, birch, oak (red or white), maple, or teak, all unfinished or prefinished. Strip flooring ranges from 1½ to 2¼ inches wide, and plank flooring is usually 3 to 8 inches wide. Parquet is a mosaic treatment of different sized pieces of wood. Wood floors range in color from light oak, which is pale gold in appearance, through medium shades of brown, to the deeper shades of black walnut or stained oak. Combinations of light and dark tones are frequently most attractive.

Wood block are patterns preassembled to facilitate installation, and they vary in size from 6 11/32 inches square to 19 inches square, or rectangles approximately 15 x 19 inches. There are patterns in herringbone, basketweave, parallel strips of uniform size running in the same direction, small squares, and various combinations (see Plate 21).

The finishing of wood flooring will depend upon the kind of wood used. Since the cellular structure of wood varies according to species, the finishing process will depend upon the material at hand. For a clear finish, a sealer should be used; it will penetrate the wood and actually enter the grain, adding strength and hardness to the surface. A floor that does not require filler may be finished by the application of stain (usually used for oak floors), followed by sanding. Next a thin coat of shellac is applied. The floor is then given another sanding, a second coat of shellac, and a final sanding. A coat of paste wax, which is applied about fifteen hours later, will supply a polish.

Light-colored floors may be finished as follows: Wood filler is rubbed into the grain and rubbed off after about twenty minutes, a thin coat of white shellac is applied, and the floor is sanded. A final coat of floor varnish thinned with turpentine is then applied. The color of the finished floor will, of course, depend upon the color of the wood that is used.

CEILINGS

Plaster ceilings may, of course, be painted any color. For example, they may be painted a pale tone of the adjoining wall color, or perhaps a dark tone if they are unusually high or if there are pipes which cannot otherwise be masked. Wallpaper applied on a high ceiling is often very effective, but this technique must be studied carefully to avoid a closed-in or heavy feeling. Wallpaper is also useful to give unity to rooms with slanted ceilings or dormers.

Ceilings that are treated acoustically are a different matter. Although there is always a temptation to paint acoustic tile, any additional paint severely reduces the acoustic quality and should therefore be avoided.

Acoustic material is divided into two categories:

1. That in which the acoustic material is formed into squares or rectangles and applied directly to the ceiling

2. That in which the acoustic material is placed inside metal grids

Acoustic material, usually warm white in color for a reflectance of 75 or more, is patterned in various ways—to imitate travertine, for example, or notched to form a pattern to collect the noise and dissipate it. Tiles 12 inches square are usually used when the material is applied directly to the ceiling, but larger sizes are used in suspended ceilings. As the asbestos tiles have paint, film, or glass-cloth finishes, their resistance to soil and ease of maintenance are increased. Metal grids hung from the structural ceiling form the obvious ceiling finish, and the acoustic material is placed in these grids. This type of installation is particularly advantageous in places where moisture or maintenance are serious problems (e.g., in food-preparation areas). Such ceilings will often incorporate heating, air conditioning, and lighting systems. The metal grids can be obtained in standard painted finishes, stainless steel, or custom colors. There are numerous variations for installation of this type of acoustic material.

Where noise is a great problem and acoustic ceilings are not the answer, it is sometimes advisable to combine utility and beauty by fastening colored carpet material to the ceiling.

Translucent ceiling systems consist of sheets of glass or plastic material that diffuse light emitted from bulbs or tubes between the translucent ceiling and the structural ceiling. These can provide dramatic effects. The color given off by such a ceiling will, of course, depend upon the color of the lighting used and the type of diffuser used; this must be given careful study (see Chapter 2, "The Effect of Light on Color").

Some ceiling systems are constructed so that they have the appearance of a series of coffers. With this type of ceiling, light is provided at the top of some or all of the coffers, and the lighting source is, therefore, obscured. Such ceiling coffers are sometimes alternated with flat areas of acoustic material; variations in color and tone are thereby obtained.

chapter seven

THE APPLICATION OF COLOR: FURNITURE

The design and construction of furniture is probably one of the oldest arts. In ancient Egypt, furniture of wood was inlaid with ivory and ebony, and gold ornament was often applied. Numerous pieces of furniture used by the ancient Greeks and Romans show a use of wood as well as bronze, marble, and iron. The forms were, to a great extent, architectural in character, and like many works of architecture they were sometimes carved and painted. Tables richly decorated with bronze, precious metals, and marble and frequently inlaid with wood, ivory, and mosaic were used in Pompeii. Like the Romans and the Greeks, the Pompeians dined while in a reclining position, and their couches were usually decorated with colorful tapestries and cushions—the first use of upholstery.

During the Gothic period, furniture was for the most part made of wood and was heavy in proportion and detail. Again, the ornament was architecturally inspired: Motifs included Gothic arches, buttresses, crockets, etc. While the furniture of ancient Egypt, Greece, and Rome was mainly designed to be used in one place, Gothic furniture was designed to be movable. Chairs, for instance, were basically chests that could be easily moved in case of political turmoil. Because of the relatively cold climate, beds were large and enclosed with a canopy and curtains. Tables and chairs were of the trestle type so that they could be dismantled and quickly moved if necessary.

During the Italian Renaissance, furniture was rich in color and, for the most part, massive. In the homes of the wealthy, at least, it was more plentiful than in earlier periods. Beds continued to be large, and were often carved and painted; tables were plain or carved, and were made in many sizes. Furniture for the display of art, such as pedestal supports for statues and ornaments, writing cabinets, and storage cabinets were used, as well as framed mirrors and pictures—all of which reflected the artistic appreciation of the times. Hand carvings and paintings were common in establishments of the wealthy. A large group of artisans was developed for this work; some of them were later imported to France by Francis I and subsequent French rulers.

In France, the Gothic period remained in vogue for some time, and furniture was similar to that used in Italy. Under Louis XIV a guild of cabinetmakers was formed by Le Brun and directed to create new and beautiful furniture. These and later groups developed the various kinds and styles of furniture that were the precursors of modern furniture. Now the furniture became more comfortable, and it was upholstered or cushioned with the magnificent fabrics of France.

The furniture of the Early Renaissance in England was developed from the Gothic styles and those of the Italian Renaissance. At first it was heavy in character. The main pieces were wardrobes, dressers, chests, chairs, tables, stools, and beds. The wood was sometimes enriched by surface grooving, and coats of arms were used. Generally the early furniture, such as that of the Elizabethan period, was heavy in proportion. During the reign of Charles II, furniture became more comfortable, and Flemish scrollwork was popular. Now cushions and upholstery became more elaborate and brilliant in color. During the William and Mary period, wood veneer came into wide use, and great attention was given to the beauty of the graining in wood pieces. Upholstery materials of all kinds continued to be used. During the Queen Anne and Early Georgian periods, furniture became finer in detail, and the beauty of veneering and grain continued to receive great attention.

Under Sir Christopher Wren, Abraham Swan, and Batty Langley, classical architectural elements were introduced, and the curved line in structural and panel forms was gradually eliminated. Mahogany continued to be used in cabinetmaking; solid mahogany was often used instead of veneering. Chippendale furniture, which was made famous by Thomas Chippendale's *Gentleman and Cabinet Maker's Director* (1754), for the most part evinced the more refined furniture styling of the time. Designs were taken from many sources, usually made in mahogany, and Chinese-inspired designs were given the name "Chinese Chippendale."

While other books of furniture designs predated and postdated those of Chippendale, none had quite so widespread an effect. George Hepplewhite's *Cabinetmakers' and Upholsterers' Guide*, which stressed slender proportions, also stressed such surface enrichment as painting and the use of satinwood. Carved ornament was often used. In 1790, Sheraton's *Cabinet-maker and Upholsterer's Drawing Book*, which contained styles that were borrowed from many sources, was published. This book stressed the straight line and the segmental curve, and had a profound effect on the designers of England and the United States. During the Adam, or Neoclassic, period, a deliberate effort was made to unify interiors by making all elements and objects in them of a single style.

The interiors of smaller houses in the late eighteenth century were sparsely furnished, and upholstery was not often used. This austerity was carried over into the simple homes in early America. During the Regency period few new ideas appeared. The style of the French Empire period had its effect on English designs, but the simple, clean lines of the styles immediately preceding it seem not to have been popular, and styles of former periods were often used. Designers seeking new and simple designs reached back into Greek antiquity for their forms and ornaments. Simplicity, however, was soon washed away during the Victorian period by the flood of clumsily designed, ornamented, and manufactured furniture, the forms of which were badly copied from Italian, Turkish, and Greek sources as well as from the entire Gothic spectrum.

As mentioned in Chapter 5, the furniture of the early periods of the United States was influenced greatly by that of the various lands from which the individual settlers had come. For the most part, the furniture was practical and useful, much of it made of wood. Since the average household could not afford many pieces of furniture, the various items—the table chair, for instance—were made to do more than one job.

Much of the fine furniture of the Georgian period in the early eighteenth century was either imported from England or made by craftsmen who had emigrated from that land. Inspired by the work of the many cabinetmakers in England and by their cabinetmaking books, the wealthy householder sought to obtain richer furniture for his home. The Philadelphia school, craftsmen who gathered in Philadelphia between 1742 and 1796, produced many fine pieces, while a similar group in Newport, Rhode Island, including John Goddard and John Townsend, produced fine examples of the blockfront type. Similar groups sprang up in other areas.

During the Federal period (1780–1830) professional architects began to work in the United States for the first time—John McComb in New York, Thomas Jefferson in Virginia, Benjamin Latrobe in Washington, Sam McIntire in Salem, and James Hoban in South Carolina. The delicacy of their work demanded equally delicate furniture, and while the Adam influence was more apparent in interior design than in furniture, the Hepplewhite designs seemed to have been particularly popular at this time. Similarly, the graceful work of Duncan Phyfe, produced between 1790 and 1830 in New York, usually in mahogany, seems to have been often used. During the American Eagle period (1812) patriotism was symbolized in furniture and other arts by the use of the eagle. This form appeared on numerous items, including picture frames, clocks, and wall brackets.

During the American Victorian period, Gothic forms again came into prominence, and it was not until the Philadelphia Exposition of 1876 that the public was ready for finer furniture. At the end of the nineteenth century, Americans who traveled in Europe or read art periodicals which displayed antiques again became enamored of antiques and brought many to this country. This practice continues today; one often places an antique piece in an otherwise contemporary room.

CASE PIECES

The wood finishes of today's furniture depend upon availability as well as the workability of the species at hand and the personal tastes of the designer and client. Walnut seems to have retained its popularity since the Italian Renaissance. During the French Renaissance oak, walnut, and poplar were used. During the eighteenth century, interiors were rich and colorful; ebony, oak, sycamore, chestnut, wildwood, kingwood, amaranth, and fruitwoods such as apple, pear, and cherry were used in marquetry. Mahogany was widely used during the middle of the eighteenth century when Chippendale produced his enduring designs, and Hepplewhite popularized the use of satinwood.

In the early days of colonial America, mahogany, which was then popular in England, was used not only in pieces imported from England but also in those made by English craftsmen who had come to the United States.

The finishes of early American mahogany furniture ranged in color from medium orange brown through yellow brown, gray brown, and reddish brown. These are imitated today by furniture manufacturers who specialize in reproducing pieces reminiscent of the past.

Walnut is widely used by wood-furniture manufacturers today. It varies in shade from a gray brown to a reddish brown or yellowish brown. There are a number of ways to finish walnut furniture. Oil-finish walnut has a mat appearance, while lacquer finish has a sheen. The number of woods and wood finishes that are available in today's market will vary from manufacturer to manufacturer. A casual walk through one showroom reveals that walnut, teak, ebony, cherry, maple, myrtle burl, and oak are available; some pieces are finished in black or chinese-red lacquer. In another showroom one sees three kinds of rosewood finishes, one type being brownish, another reddish brown, and the third a lacquer which has an orange appearance. This showroom's mahogany is available in dark gray brown, pinkish brown, and gray-yellow brown, and its teak varies in color from dull gray tan to gray orange to deep gray brown. It also exhibits furniture made of a scrubbed rosewood, which is a weatherbeaten light gray in quality.

Most manufacturers find it expedient to limit the number of colors and finishes. For example, one of the larger manufacturers of case pieces specializes in redwood, walnut, rosewood, teak, and oak; another limits its finishes to mat-finish teak, oiled walnut, oiled ash, and rosewood; still another offers only walnut. Some showrooms display only one kind of wood.

For additional beauty and color, as well as grain contrast, designers sometimes use several different kinds of wood, faintly reminiscent of marquetry, in one piece of furniture. Glass, marble, travertine, and leather are often used too for the tops of desks, tables, and chests to add interest.

Metals, such as stainless steel, brushed or polished chrome, or anodized aluminum, are frequently combined with wood in the framing of chairs, tables, and cabinets. New materials such as clear plastic are also employed to add to the diversity.

In addition to the natural or stained finishes used with wood, painted finishes have long been popular. In the time of Louis XVI cream or ivory, gold, sky blue, yellow, gray, rose, and apricot were popular. Occasionally landscapes or other scenes were painted on panels for added adornment. During Colonial times in the United States, the art of stenciling was popular and colorfully used. The Hitchcock chair is available today in reproductions in colors such as barn red, country yellow, hemlock green, greenwich blue, or antique white. Wood

FIG. 7.1   Dining Room, Private Residence
Ezra Stoller (ESTO), Photographer

can also be finished in colored lacquer in a tortoiseshell pattern or in color in the Oriental manner. The Oriental lacquer finishes are beautiful in all shades of red—from bright and clear to soft and winey, accented with gold. Shades of green or black, also decorated with gold, are also very popular.

Rattan, reed, or wicker furniture is often finished in colors such as pebble, antique white, pink, gold, green willow, sunset red, malacca, pecan, black, teak, or smoke.

Contemporary designs in plastic materials are obtainable in clear bright shades of blue, red, beige, green, orange, or white and are extremely useful for introducing color into what might otherwise be a humdrum environment.

CONTRACT FURNITURE

The design and furnishing of institutional and commercial interiors plays an important part in our well-being; this is recognized by management and public alike. An orderly, attractive environment is an asset whether it is an office, a hospital room, a bank, or a detention facility, and color plays a major role in creating such an atmosphere.

Manufacturers of furniture for these spaces, in contrast with that designed for residential use, have developed designs and finishes which are attractive, convenient, and long-lasting. Wood pieces are available in various species, including walnut, mahogany, pine, oak, teak, and elm, in finishes from light to dark. Many times plastic laminates are used for tops of wood or metal bases of desks, tables, and chests. Some imitate the wood tones while others are in solid colors. Sophisticated pieces for executive or other special areas are available in such exotic woods as mahogany, rosewood, or ebony. Occasionally two kinds of wood are used, or the tops are of marble, glass, travertine, leather, or other material.

Stainless steel, brushed or polished chrome, and aluminum in various finishes are frequently combined with wood.

Metal alone or in combination with plastic laminate is widely used in the manufacture of desks, files, chairs, beds, and tables, and these are available in colors such as beige, sand, ivory, red, terra-cotta, green, or gold, to be used singly or in combination.

Designers and manufacturers have made great progress in developing flexible, well-proportioned, special-purpose furniture for the requirements of commercial and institutional situations. In an open office situation where, not too long ago, possibly thirty or forty desks of dull gray or olive green steel were arranged unimaginatively row upon row, with attendant clutter and confusion, and much to the employees' discomfort, it is now possible through a system that uses "landscaping" or "work stations" (see Plates 22a and 22b) to provide partial enclosures for each occupant. A typical solution might be a beige acoustic panel with a mat acrylic enamel finish or fabric cover. To this might be attached a desk with a wood-patterned plastic laminate top. Such a work station would contain the files, compartments, bookshelves, and light required for the particular job to be accomplished. Properly planned, the formerly drab area becomes colorful and efficient for the same number of workers as formerly occupied the open space. These systems are very flexible, and if changes occur in operations it is not a major problem or expense to make the required alterations.

UPHOLSTERED FURNITURE

The designs of chairs and sofas evolved at a rather slow pace until the beginning of the so-called "functional" era, when it seems to have suddenly occurred

FIG. 7.2 Hunting Lodge
Tom Lee, A.S.I.D., Designer
Champion International, Building Products Division, Stamford, CT

to designers that furniture should be designed to fit the human anatomy. While the first attempts at functional seating design did not bring forth especially good results, there are today dozens of designs which successfully break from the past in form and construction. While wood continues to be used for the frames of much of our furniture, other materials are being used. For instance, one finds steel bases, as on Peter Hoyte's "Orbit" chair; tubular steel construction with foam-rubber cushions, as in Eva Hauser's Swedish rocker; and enamel or chrome-finish steel frames, as in Robin Cruikshank's "DC-102" dining chair. Eero Saarinen's "Tulip" chair is made of plastic and cast aluminum; molded plywood is used by Charles Eames in his armchair and footstool, which have down-filled hide cushions and bases of steel and aluminum. The famous Barcelona chair, designed in 1929 for the Barcelona Exhibition by Ludwig Miës van der Rohe, has a polished steel frame, hide straps, and buttoned hide-covered cushions. Other very comfortable form-fitting chairs with frames of laminated plywood include Alvar Aalto's Finnish cantilever easy chair, designed in 1935. The "Egg" chair of Arne Jacobsen employs light plastic for the frame and a covering of foam rubber.

While most of these chairs use materials which we have mentioned before, the form of each chair or sofa dictates to the designer the kind of fabric it will accept. Chairs of the great contemporary designers seem to achieve a clean, architectural appearance when upholstered in black, white, olive, deep gray, or tan leather. These colors accentuate the clean sculptural quality and exquisite lines of chairs. Smaller and more playful chair designs will often accept fabrics in colorful solids, stripes, and geometrics.

Sofas, while occasionally used for scale and balance, are predominantly considered in terms of comfort, and the down-filled pillows formerly used to achieve this goal were a good solution. Decorative pillows are always an attractive accessory, but improved design and proportion have added greatly to the inherent comfort of the sofa. There are many lean tailored designs available which can be covered in virtually any type of fabric, including the very substantial acrylic-backed fabrics developed for contract use. There is also a trend toward bulkier types, due to the development of synthetic fillers which are economical as well as comfortable when compared with expensive down or feathers. This trend toward softer designs leads to the use of softer fabrics such as velvets and printed fabrics (see Plates 24 and 25).

Fabrics

One of the largest and most varied sources of color available to the architect and interior designer for interior work is the field of fabrics. A sampling of the racks in a decorative-fabric showroom will make the beholder aware of the fact that there are many different kinds available; more appear every day. In the past, the words "medium-weight upholstery covering" described cotton, linen, and silk in brocades, chintz, cretonne, crewel embroidery, moire, damask, satin, sateen, and taffeta. Heavyweight fabrics included crewel embroidery, mohair, brocatelle, damask, monk's cloth, petit point, twill, velvet velour, velveteen, and lampas. Today these fabrics are still available, but there is also a host of new fabrics, including many composed of synthetic fibers. Many fibers are blends of several different fibers designed to increase resistance to wear and often enhance their beauty. Fabrics are available in solids, mixtures, stripes, and printed designs.

It should be remembered that the colors of traditional fabrics were determined by the materials available, the technical limitations of the times, the taste of the society in which they were developed, and the light in which they were to be used. One may see in traditional fabrics a great many subtleties, nuances, and details that can only be understood and appreciated if they are properly used in today's interiors. While it is possible to use contemporary fabrics in traditional interiors (or vice versa), a great deal of experience in color is required. The interiors of a courthouse built in, say, 1837, in which there are finely studied architectural interior details, will be complemented by damasks which are reproduced from authentic designs of the same period. There are

(a)

(b)

15. (a) Ceramic tile design for residence, Southampton, New York
    (b) Enclosed patio using ceramic tile flooring

American Olean Tile Company, Lansdale, PA

16. (a) Area rug, "Chinoiserie"

Daren Pierce/Inman Cook, Designers

(b) Wall hanging, "Conversation Piece"

Burt Groedel, Artist
Edward Fields, Inc., New York, NY

(a)

(b)

17. Living room
Zephyr blue Anso nylon carpet

Bigelow-Sanford, Inc., Greenville, SC

18. Reception areas with Corlon Quiet Zone II
   (a) Random Texture
   (b) Grand Central

*Armstrong Cork Company,
Lancaster, PA*

(a)

(b)

19. Sitting room
GAF Brite-Bond adhesive-backed floor tile

GAF Corporation, Floor Products, New York, NY

20. Kitchen
Gafstar Softred sheet vinyl, "Calgary" pattern

GAF Corporation, Floor Products, New York, NY

Standard BondWood, par (select) red oak

Basketweave BondWood, par and better red oak, shown natur

Saxony BondWood, black walnut, shown natural

Canterbury BondWood, par and better white oak, shown natu

Herringbone BondWood, par and better angelique teak, shown natural

Domino BondWood, par and better white oak, stained

21. Patterns of wood flooring

Harris Manufacturing Company, Johnson City, TN

22. **Two office areas using open-plan components**
Steelcase, Inc., Grand Rapids, MI

23. **Executive office**
Steelcase, Inc., Grand Rapids, MI

24. Sofa upholstered in print fabric

Elroy Edson, A.S.I.D., Designer
Selig Manufacturing Company, Inc., Leominster, MA

25. Living Room

Elroy Edson, A.S.I.D., Designer
Selig Manufacturing Company, Inc., Leominster, MA

26. Fabric samples
(a) Shibui Collection
(b) Naturals Collection

Boris Kroll Fabrics, Inc., New York, NY

27. Living room in restored house
Peg Walker, Designer
Breneman, Inc., Cincinnati, OH

28. Studio apartment

Michael Sherman, Designer
Breneman, Inc., Cincinnati, OH

29. Living room

David Eugene Bell, A.S.I.D., Designer
Window Shade Manufacturers Association, New York, NY

30. Area rug in reception lobby

*Interior designed by Designers Collaborative, Joan Blutter
and Joyce Vagasy, Chicago, IL*

*Sketch from SURROUND, prepared for the Wool Bureau, Inc.,
by David Singer Associates, New York, NY*

31. Office Area

*Interior designed by Designers Collaborative, Joan Blutter
and Joyce Vagasy, Chicago, IL*

*Sketch from SURROUND, prepared by for the Wool Bureau, Inc.,
by David Singer Associates, New York, NY*

32. Somerset Inn, Troy, Michigan

Volk & London, Architects
American Olean Tile Company, Lansdale, PA

33. Monroe C. Gutman Library, Harvard University,
Cambridge, Massachusetts

Benjamin Thompson & Associates, Architects
Ezra Stoller (ESTO), Photographer

34. Mount Healthy School, Columbus, Indiana

Hardy Holzman Pfeiffer Associates, Architects
Norman McGrath, Photographer

35. Fifth Street Subway Station, Philadelphia

Ueland and Junker, Architects
Lawrence S. Williams, Inc., Photographer

many "restoration" fabrics on the market which reproduce the designs and colors of the several historical periods. Typically, damasks of our Colonial times are available in tan gold, cream gold, blue green, yellow green, brilliant red, and soft gray blue. The color scheme of an office done in the Colonial style might include curtains of a documentary print with a gray-beige background and a blue-green tree pattern, one chair in the same fabric, a deep red desk chair, medium green side chairs, and a beige carpet.

A bedroom in the French tradition might include a small white, pink, and slate-blue cotton print with headboard, canopy, bedspread, and upholstered chairs all done in the same fabric.

English chintzes in the traditional style are also extremely popular. One with red and deep blue flowers on a natural-white background can be used for curtains, with the sofa in bronze green and an accent of blue on a chair.

Interestingly enough, many clients request period design, style, and color, probably because they feel that it gives them a cultural link with the past. At the other end of the scale, however, an increasing number of clients are asking for modern upholstery and curtain fabrics that are in keeping with the architecture of today. The designers of period rooms often use soft pastel blendings, while those who produce contemporary rooms achieve their aims by making bold statements in color. In a typical contemporary interior one may see a great many brilliant colors on plain, striped, or geometric-patterned fabrics, woven and printed. Stripes of narrow or varying widths might include almost primary hues such as light and dark blue, orange brown and red, red and blue, blue and green, orange and yellow, or orange and black. One may use a bright spectrum-blue sofa with a bright green chair, or a beige sofa with bright yellow and blue pillows on it. In rooms where brilliant upholstery colors are used, accessories of black, white, olive, putty, deep blue gray, purple, plum, and gray are used as counterpoints.

Contemporary fabrics offer many interesting color combinations and effects when blended, and they are available in a variety of fascinating weaves which range from very lightweight to nubby and heavy fabrics.

A striped upholstery fabric of 100 percent nylon is offered by F. Schumacher & Company of New York. The stripe is approximately 1 inch wide, but the widths of each color are varied for a pleasing effect. Some of the color combinations are as follows:

> Light and deep blue with light brown
> Natural and tan
> Garnet, beige, and olive green
> Copper, black, and Spanish red
> Deep orange, purple, and deep red
> Deep tan, black, and rust

Another upholstery fabric available through Schumacher contains 45 percent wool, 30 percent nylon, and 25 percent cotton, with acrylic backing. The stripe is approximately 7¼ inches in width, and the colors are spaced in varying widths for interesting effects:

> Bright yellow, orange, and green
> Beige, rust, tan, and black
> Rust, bright blue, black, and gray

Medium blue, neutral gray, emerald, and strong yellow
Deep yellow, rust, green, and bright blue
Olive green, lavender, neutral gray, and light copper

A collection of 100 percent wool fabrics in neutral colors with varying weaves is offered in combinations of charcoal brown and white, gray and white, banker's gray, random oatmeal and brown, brown and beige, or beige and sand. A wool plush fabric of 32 percent cotton, 36 percent viscose rayon, and 32 percent wool is available in gold, yellow, blue, brown, camel, eggplant, bright green, pine, lacquer, russet, and copper.

In addition to the wide variety of fabrics for upholstery, special fabrics are produced just for use as curtains. These are usually light in weight and loosely woven, or woven of fine yarn for a sheer appearance. Linen, cotton, and silk have long been used, but modern requirements have brought about synthetic fibers such as nylon, acrylic, Fiberglas, or Verel, which are easily maintained; Fiberglas and Verel, among others, are considered flame resistant in that they do not support combustion.

A recent offering by Schumacher of a line of lightweight printed fabrics has the following attributes, for example: It is machine washable (subject to minimum shrinkage and requiring only light touch-up with an iron), dry cleanable, abrasion resistant, and flame resistant. The material is woven with 75 percent "Leavil," 17 percent polyester, and 8 percent linen, and the collection uses colors in clear or muted tones with geometric and floral prints. The available color combinations include brown, gold, black, and green as well as olive, light blue, and persimmon on off-white fabric, and olive, both light and dark, yellow-gold, and white.

In addition to the clearly defined traditional and contemporary upholstery fabrics, one finds fabrics which are traditionally inspired but modern in feeling woven on jacquard looms. Boris Kroll Fabrics presents a group of fabrics for residential use in their Shibui collection (Plate 26a). The collection includes damasks, stripes, small all-over patterns, striaes, and solid fabrics designed so that they coordinate with each other by pattern as well as color. Another fabric design, Pirate, for contract use, is a twill of 75 percent wool and 25 percent nylon, engineered for best abrasion resistance and durability. It is available in fourteen stock colors and can be custom dyed. The stock colors include:

Brick	Amber	Navy	Mulberry	Rust
Toast	Seal	Teal	Terra-cotta	Fawn
Mocha	Black	Copen	Vermilion	

In their naturals collection (Plate 26b), the combination of 70 percent virgin natural undyed neutral colored wool fibers with 30 percent virgin nylon staple creates superb textural effects.

Each designer tends to favor a particular segment of taste, but of course there are many fabrics available for those who occupy a position between the extremes.

Textile dyeing All fabrics were at one time colored with vegetable dyes. Today most fabrics are dyed with less expensive synthetic dyes. A partial list[1]

---

[1] *Encyclopedia of Textiles*, American Fabrics Magazine, ed., Englewood Cliffs, NJ: Prentice-Hall, Inc., 1960, pp. 469–471.

FIG. 7.3   Hotel Restaurant
Courtesy of William Pahlmann, F.A.S.I.D.

of dyes is given below, but it must be remembered that chemists are continually inventing more brilliant and light- and washfast dyes and new dyes for new synthetic fabrics.

Dye	Qualities	Fabrics
Vegetable extract dyes (also dyes from animals and minerals)	Limited range of colors. Expensive.	All
Basic dyes (Organic base soluble in simple acid)	Not always colorfast. Give brilliant color.	Hemp, linen, silk, wool; also cotton and rayon when binding agent is added.
Direct dyes	More lightfast and not resistant to loss of color by washing. Less brilliant than basic dyes. Wide color range*.	Cotton, linen, cellulose rayon, wool, silk, nylon
Acid dyes (Napthol or azo dyes)	Produce bright, colorfast reds.	Nylon, silk, wool piecegoods

FIG. 7.4 Living Room, Private Residence
Carol Eichen, Decorator
National Association of Mirror Manufacturers, Washington, DC

Dye	Qualities	Fabrics
Sulfur dyes	Poor resistance to sunlight. Color not brilliant. Weakens structure of some fabrics.	Cotton, linen, cellulose rayons
Vat dyes (Made from anthraquinone, carbazole, and indigo)	Very lightfast. Washfast. Most durable of dyes.	Cotton, linen, rayon, silk, wool, all types of fibers
Acetate dyes	Produce brilliant colors.	Useful on synthetic fibers, especially nylon
Alizarin dyes (synthetically produced)	Produce bright, dark red, as well as other colors.	Wool, sometimes cotton
Aniline dyes	Usually used to obtain black. Lightfast. Washfast.	Cotton
Azoic dyes (from aromatic hydrocarbons)	Lightfast. Wetfast.	Dacron

Dye	Qualities	Fabrics
Chrome dyes	Very light- and washfast.	Woolens, worsteds
Developed dyes	Produce same shades as direct dyes, but more fade-resistant.	Cotton, rayon
Neutral dyes Similar to chrome dyes, but metal salts are mixed in before use	Flat, drab colors.	Wool; synthetics such as nylon

Dyeing Processes The following processes are used on yarns:[2]

Process	Description	Yarn	Finished product
Stock dyeing	Fibers are completely immersed prior to spinning or blending. Economical only for quantities in excess of 5,000 lbs.	Mixtures, blends, and unusual and rich cloths	Good color. Lightfast
Top dyeing	Thread-like fibers are combed and wound on tops, then immersed in tanks, where dye is forced through fibers.	Worsted fabrics	Dyed thread suitable for blending of colors. Lightfast if dye is premetalized.*
Solution dyeing	Dyeing occurs while fiber material is in liquid state.	Synthetic fibers	Good color. Excellent lightfastness.
Yarn dyeing	Yarn is immersed in dye solution and turned to force dye through it.	Any fiber in yarn form	Lightfastness can be adjusted to end use of fabric.
Color space dyeing	Yarn is colored at prescribed intervals along its length.	Nylon	Light- and washfast. Multicolored for random effects.

* Susheela Dantyagi, *Fundamentals of Textiles and Their Care*, Bombay: Orient Longmans, Ltd., 1964.

CIBA Chemical and Dye Company (Div. of CIBA Corporation).

The following dyeing processes are used on woven fabric:[3]

Process	Description	Fabric	Finished Product
Piece dyeing	Lengths of "gray" goods are immersed in dye enough times to obtain required brightness. Economical for small quantities.	Woven	True in color
Union dyeing	A one-bath process in which the same color is made to penetrate different yarns or fibers.	Combinations of yarns, such as wool worsted and orlon	Different yarns or fibers are the same color
Cross dyeing	A form of union dyeing which permits the dyeing of more than one color in a fabric woven of different fibers: one fiber resists the penetration of certain colors while others absorb them.	Dacron, rayon, acrylic in combination with (for example) wool	Multicolored

[2] Ibid., p. 475.

[3] Ibid., p. 477.

Textile Printing Man has applied colored designs to the surface of fabrics since earliest times, and printed fabrics are still widely used today. Below is a brief description of textile-printing methods:[4]

Process	Description	Area of Use
Resist printing	Areas not to be colored are covered with substance which resists dye. After dyeing, resist is removed; undyed portion is left as is or is colored by direct printing.	Ancient Egypt as early as 600 B.C. India Java Peru Indonesia
Wood block printing	Design is carved in reverse on surface of wood blocks, then printed by applying colored dye to each block and pressing each block to surface of fabric in correct sequence.	China, eighth century Egypt, fifth century Italy, twelfth century Germany (Rhine area) thirteenth and fourteenth centuries
Roller printing	Design is printed with engraved metal rollers, one color per roller. This method was at first limited to one color, but today many colors can be applied with great speed.	England and France, 1780 to present
Screen printing	One screen, of silk, nylon, or metal thread, is used for each color in a design. Portion of pattern to be colored is cut out of masking film placed on screen. Color is applied to fabric by brushing or squeezing it through cutout portion of film. Successive screens are for each color. Formerly a hand operation, this method is now mechanized for rapid, accurate production.	France, mid-nineteenth century to present

Printing methods today vary according to location. The older methods are still used where labor is plentiful. But most textile printing is now done by the roller machine, whose great speed makes the finished article relatively inexpensive. The decorative-fabric trade still has a number of small printing establishments where handprinted fabrics are produced. The range in size of pattern, color, and shading is far greater in hand-printed fabrics than in roller-printed materials, but the cost is also higher.

Leather

Leather is often used for upholstery, and its beauty, like that of all natural materials, is in the variation of its color and texture. Unlike many other natural materials, however, leather must be put through a long and laborious process before it is ready for use: curing, trimming, washing, fleshing, bating, tanning, rolling, slicing, soaking, drying, finishing, softening, and finally dyeing. The architect or interior designer must be aware of the fact that the best hides are selected hides which have been gently sanded, or "snuffed," to remove marks or imperfections such as wire scratches and hair marks that were made during

[4] Ibid., pp. 479–499.

the life of the animal. These hides are termed *top-grain leathers*. For medium-priced furniture, leathers which are cut out of the hide just below the top grain are used. They are known as *deep buff leathers*.

The dyeing of leather is a high art. The colors are kept quite constant by spraying the leathers with dyes made to exact formulas. The number of colors that are available for upholstery will depend upon the manufacturer; some lines offer as many as 100. One representative line offers these thirty-one colors:

White	Larkspur blue
Bottle green	Turquoise
Medium yellow green	Light blue
Medium blue green	Tobacco brown
Olive green	Tan
Celadon green	Light rust
Deep fuchsia	Tangerine
Pinkish red	Golden yellow
Pink	Pale yellow
French ultramarine blue	Bittersweet
Cornflower blue	Deep greenish gold
Cerulean blue	Warm rust
Sand	Tan brown
Charcoal gray	Sable brown
Deep red	Lemon yellow
Black	

Before placing an order for a piece of furniture which is to be covered with leather, the architect or interior designer should ask for a color-selection card so that he or she will know whether the desired color is available, or whether a custom color is needed. A rich tangerine, for instance, may not be available in a limited selection. The larger selections, of course, will include a number of shades of each color, and the larger the selection the greater the possibility that subtlety can be obtained. Some manufacturers provide custom colors at additional expense.

In addition to monotone colors and finishes, a number of top-grain leathers are available in two-tone effects which are given a patina. An examination of a rather extensive line will show that these are available in deep reds, gray green, tan, black, gunmetal, yellow green, tortoiseshell, and deep green. In still another group, a whitish glaze is given to yellow, pink, tan, gray, green, blue, and turquoise to produce a more pastel shade.

Leather may also be used for the tops of tables and desks or chests, as well as on doors. Pigskin has been used for flooring and wall covering. Leather in 6- by 6-inch or 12- by 12-inch tiles, mounted on a warp-free board, is available for use on walls. The leather usually has a gold-tooled design which is most effective.

Vinyl

While the early vinyls used for upholstery attempted to imitate leather colors, the manufacturers have now developed a range of colors and finishes all their own. For the most part, no attempt is made to copy the natural imperfections of leather: Vinyl is treated frankly and honestly as a new material with its own exciting possibilities and uses. One of the lines recently introduced contains sixty-four colors which run the gamut from grayed colors to those of great brilliance. The color names themselves are descriptive and easily remembered: hyacinth, loganberry, raspberry, red apple, mandarin orange, tiger lily, fern, bluebell, etc.

Material for upholstery must be of a heavier weight than that usually used for walls; it is also advisable to select a rubber or stretch fabric that will "breathe." Manufacturers usually specify the uses for which their product is suited, and these recommendations should be heeded.

In addition to plain vinyls, embossed, printed, and "woven" patterns are available in a variety of colors. There are reptile patterns; fabric patterns such as *matelassé*, linen, moire, and burlap; self-stripe (two different textures on a single-color material); rough textures, such as straw; and even a quilted pattern.

SCREENS AND ROOM DIVIDERS

Portable screens, many of which combine utility with beauty, have been used for centuries in the Orient and in Europe. Varying in shape, color, and design according to origin, they at once provide a sense of privacy and a means for artistic expression. Perhaps the best-known and most expensive is the Chinese coromandel, notable for its carved intaglio design. Most often it is black, but sometimes it is brown or dark red, with the intaglio treated with gold or silver metallics or with color. Genuine antique coromandel screens are rare, and most of those made prior to the eighteenth century are in museums. Reproductions are available. Often the coromandel will be in panels 18 inches wide and up to 12 feet high.

Screens are frequently covered in antique French or Chinese wallpapers or scenic papers, and therefore they can be adapted to their setting. Japanese screens are painted on silk grounds or other types of paper; the subject matter usually relates to the great art of Japan. Scenes include florals, trees (often bamboos), and sensitively rendered landscapes. They are usually in black wash or color.

The shoji screen of Japan is made up of a series of panels and a delicate frame of narrow wood members. The pattern, consisting of a series of rectangles, is usually horizontal but occasionally vertical. A typical rectangle in a shoji screen might measure 8⅞ by 10⅝ inches. If the screens are made by excellent Japanese craftsmen, and if dried, seasoned cedar is used, the frames around each panel will be as narrow as ¾ by 1⅛ inches, and the minor members which form the rectangles will be as small as 5⁄16 inch. Rice paper, which is translucent and is made in a number of different patterns, is applied in a sheet on the back of the shoji. Its translucence gives the shoji a light, airy appearance. In the United States, where rice paper is not as readily available and where permanence is sought, plastic material often takes the place of rice paper. It, too, is translucent, and imbedded in it and forming its pattern are long white threads, leaves of green, rust, or red, butterflies, or bamboo.

Japanese closet doors, behind which bedding is stored during the day, are

FIG. 7.5 *Dining Room with mirrored glass panels*
Carol Eichen, Decorator
National Association of Mirror Manufacturers, Washington, DC

frequently treated with distinctive wallpapers that provide restrained color and pattern. Usually the major pattern in these papers is limited to the lower portion of the closet doors, and it may consist of horizontal bands of chinese red, off-white, chartreuse, blue gray, and gold. More elaborate traditional papers include landscapes, seascapes, or leaf patterns; modern designs may include wide bands of fish swimming in a narrow band of sea. One of the most charming patterns that the author has seen consisted of a series of horizontal bands, beginning wide at the bottom and becoming steadily narrower as they approached the top. The bands were a soft shade of brown on a pale brown ground. Where color and objects are part of the pattern, they are usually tied together with a softly colored background—for instance, leaves of black and silver and white are placed on a background of golden yellow. Bronze and black fish swim in a blue green sea. A range of mountains in a band at the bottom of a pair of closet doors will often be painted in several shades, the nearer mountains dark blue green, the range immediately beyond white and gray, the most distant range pale purple.

A number of portable screens of a less restrained nature are available commercially. Most of them are made in panels of varying widths, each section being hinged to the next. Usually the frames are of wood; plastic, metal grilles, woven or carved wood, cane, fabric, or glass complete the panels. The faces may be flush or sunken.

Where wood is used, it may have a natural finish or be stained, or it may be painted in any desired color. Other screens, or room dividers, are available in molded gypsum, leaded fiber glass, beaded glass, concrete filigree, and aluminum and other metals.

Decorative beads of wood, cork, glass, or plastic can also be effectively used as room dividers. Larger beads are suitable for large areas; smaller beads can be used in smaller spaces. Plastic beads can be supplied in such transparent colors as crystal, amber, aqua, green, sapphire, rose, red, and black. Wood beads are available in standard wood tones, pastel colors, or metallic colors. Wood beads and spindles are available in natural, tan, brown, black, and white enamel. Strings of beads can be hung from curtain rods, slit rods, fabric-covered dowels, screw eyes, or moldings.

chapter eight

THE
APPLICATION OF
COLOR:
FURNISHINGS

WINDOW TREATMENTS

Curtains

Curtains were originally used on cold walls and open doorways to keep heat in. Although windows were draped in the Orient as early as the sixth century, windows in the West were not curtained until mid-Renaissance times. Early curtain textiles were brilliant in color and included velvets and brocades from the East or from the workshops of Florence. The fabrics of the Louis XIV era were for the most part florals inspired by the gardens of Versailles. In England during the reign of Queen Anne, patterns were larger than in France, and the curtains were used with wooden-based valances which were covered by matching fabric. In addition, cotton prints from India and chintz were used.

Fabric patterns have varied with architectural style. During the Rococo age, designs became irregular and curved, and the curtains themselves were in most cases unbalanced and unrestrained. During the era of Louis XIV, patterns were small, curved, and lacking in continuity. Subject matter included landscapes, flowers, plumes and feathers, and graceful female figures. During the time of Thomas Chippendale, the patterns of France included Chinese designs which were modified by French weavers. During this time also, cornices of gilt and japanned wood in an Oriental style began to be used. Elaborate curves were employed to modify bare walls, and great amounts of gold cloth, as well as fringes of gold and silver, appeared in most drapery material used in Tudor houses. France was the center of drapery fashion for the roughly 200-year period that ended with Napoleon's reign. It is interesting to note that for a while after 1660, curtains grew fuller and more luxurious-looking and reflected the king's great wealth. During this period it was usual for a single glass curtain to cover an entire window, but toward the end of the seventeenth century curtains were designed in two panels with draw cords to open and close them.

During this period, pastel colors were used in France. Typical of these was Du Barry's Blushing Rose Pink. During the time immediately before the French Revolution, ostentation in interior design was tempered by the use of less ornate designs. Bouffant draperies began to disappear; proportions and details became balanced and more restrained in tone; patterns became smaller and less flowing. The classic trend, which began after the first Louis, continued. Draperies were relatively simple, with swags draped over a metal pole, sometimes pulled through large brass rings, and ending in a cascade or flat jabot.

The colors of the Directoire period were brilliant. They included bright red, green, deep yellow, black, and white. Patterns were formal and included narrow contrasting stripes. During the period of Napoleon, curtains were designed to appear carelessly hung, but in reality it was a studied carelessness: the fabric was carefully cut to lie in beautiful fashion over ornate poles that were made to look like spears, and eagles were often placed so as to catch the fabric in their beaks.

Calico was used in informal rooms during the Empire, but in formal rooms heavy fabrics, including satins, silks, moires, and embroidered velvets, were used. Occasionally there were three sets of draperies in contrasting colors such as gold, red, and green, or orange, pink, and blue. The colors were unusually harsh at that time. By the time Napoleon fell from power, the interior designs inspired by him also fell from grace. The French designers, having worked so long at developing those motifs, suddenly found themselves out of work. So it was that England became the center of style.

During the Victorian period, draperies were similar to those of the Empire in France, but they were heavier and larger. Their main function was to keep out light. Fabrics were heavy; they included velvets and damasks, most often in gold or dark red. With the advent of cheap machine-made fabric, lace was used at all windows—even those of the poor, who had curtains for the first time. Interior window shades, which had been used up until this time, continued to be used in England and in the United States.

In the eclectic period between Victorian and Modern, draperies were made in just about every style and material. During the mid-1920s, however, the idea of draping an entire window wall became popular. With this new design, the curtains could be opened during the daytime and closed during the dark hours to give the impression of a draped wall. The architect of that period of modern construction, reaching out for new forms and new methods, had no more use for historic designs in fabrics than for historic forms in architecture. The idea was to eliminate reminders of the past, such as heavy Victorian curtains, and houses were thrown open to sunlight. Where curtains were used, they were for the purpose of privacy only. Color, pattern, and form, devices previously used in draperies, were now incorporated into the architecture itself. The architectural space became a three-dimensional colored experience. Architecture no longer depended for its success upon things applied to it, but was in itself a complete, fresh, emotional experience. Suddenly architecture related to all mankind, not only to rulers, potentates, and presidents. Suddenly, today, the designer of a contemporary house—instead of having to adhere to standard treatments—can individualize the curtain treatment of the building. If the window walls in a given design need to be treated for privacy only, a plain fabric related in color to other elements in the room is used. If the windows are located high in the wall, privacy is not a problem; no curtains are required, so they are omitted. If, on the other hand, an architectural space has been designed so that the curtains are expected to contribute to color and pattern, outer curtains are sometimes used with patterns reminiscent of famous contemporary paintings. Draperies for sun control may similarly be patterned—for example, with geometrics in oranges, brilliant greens, and blues, printed on light backgrounds. Or solid contemporary colors may be used.

The colors may be planned according to the scheme that the architect has in mind, and they may include such soft shades as gray beige, pale blue, white, or deep brilliant blues mixed with white or white and black. Sometimes curtain colors consist of alternate panels of, say, green, blue, and red. Often, of course, sheer glass curtains are used over a large glass area, while panels are used on either end of an opening.

If he wishes, the architect can substitute for draperies any number of other items—shades, bamboo blinds, vertical venetian blinds, woven aluminum blinds, etc. Contemporary architects have given themselves a magnificent new freedom: they can do anything they wish. They are no longer responsible to style makers; they make their own style. In truth, the contemporary architect, in his or her continuing quest for new forms and colors, is more responsive to human needs and wishes than architects were in almost any other period of history.

Shades and Blinds

There are, in addition to curtains, a number of other decorative means by which light may be controlled. These include venetian blinds of all kinds, woven blinds, matchstick blinds, vertical blinds, roman shades, and window shades.

The standard 2-inch aluminum-slat venetian blind is manufactured in over thirty different colors such as off-white, oyster white, ivory, gray-beige, peach, pink, pastel green, and silver, as well as quiet patterns in various colors. Tapes and cords for these blinds are available to match or blend with the slats. A wide selection of hardware and accessories allows almost any type of installation problem to be solved.

There is also a more delicate venetian blind with slats 25 millimeters (0.984 inch) wide; it has an invisible ladder rather than the outside tape on either side. Levolor Lorentzen of Hoboken, New Jersey, manufactures this "Riviera" blind in more than 100 different colors. They are also made with all white on the outside and a color on the inside, which is an ideal solution where color variations would not be pleasing on the outside of a building. The selection includes over twenty brilliant colors, and the blinds can be assembled with all one color or with a design of two or more colors for unlimited decorative effects. Plate 36 shows the Riviera blind on Polished Aluminum, Camel, and Burnt Almond.

Woven aluminum blinds Woven aluminum blinds can be used as shades, either roll-up, spring-roller, Roman, or duo-fold, and also as draperies or room dividers. Colored aluminum slats about $\frac{5}{16}$ inch wide are woven together with threads such as chenille, nylon, or cotton in different patterns and colors. A fairly simple pattern might employ slats in a pastel color such as surf green, blue sky, antique, or crystal pink woven with groups of four plain nylon threads spaced about 1 inch apart. Another version has nylon webbing about ½ inch wide as the warp and is available in watermelon, lemon yellow, crystal pink, and blue sky. More decorative effects are obtained with the use of a variety of colors and types of chenille thread. For example, a yellow blind might be woven with chenille of various sizes in shades from yellow to orange to brown, arranged in stripes about 5 inches wide spaced 8 inches apart. Other patterns combine both flat slats and rods with closely woven threads in colors such as yellow, white, gold, and green thread on bright green slats, or brown slats woven with gold, light brown, dark brown, and rust. Another variation might be brown slats woven with gray and red-orange threads.

Woven wood blinds Wood slats, reeds, and dowels are also used to make decorative window coverings when woven with various threads. They can also be employed as room dividers, folding doors, or screens. As window covers in any one of the several arrangements previously mentioned, they filter light and eliminate glare. If privacy is a necessity, a web vinyl coating can be applied.

Slats, reeds, and dowels can be of Philippine mahogany, fruitwood, walnut, satin fir, pine, and bamboo. Threads may be of chenille, cotton, nylon, and other synthetics as well as nontarnishable metallics to provide highlights in the design. Some woven wood blinds are available in stock designs in predetermined colors, or custom colors and patterns can be provided. The slats can be stained or painted and of various widths from ⅜ to 1¼ inches. The variations and color effects are practically limitless as the wood can be left visible between groups of threads, or the weaving can cover the wood entirely.

Tropicraft of San Francisco has an extensive line, and the following are examples of some of their patterns.

A stock pattern of ⅜-inch slats and reeds painted light gray with chenille threads of light turquoise in bands of varying widths spaced approximately 5 inches apart, with occasional gold thread.

A lightly woven pattern containing dowels only, painted off-white, with white cotton thread.

A custom pattern having ¾-inch slats alternated with two reeds, stained walnut and heavily woven in varied-width stripes of chenille, rust, gold, metallic braid, copper, charcoal gray, and black.

A pattern similar to the above solidly woven in chenille in stripes of red, black, gold, and white.

A custom pattern of ¾-inch slats and reeds painted medium blue, solidly woven with stripes of red and white with accent of gold Lurex.

A custom pattern of ¾-inch slats and dowels stained walnut and woven with bands of varying widths containing ½-inch wool felt in blue, accents of red wool, blue and brown chenille, and gray chenille.

An all-reed design woven solidly in white Acrilan thread.

Window shades The contemporary window shade remains one of the most widely used and inexpensive methods of controlling light. The most popular roller shade is available in colors such as white, gray, and ivory in translucent and opaque styles of vinyl-coated cloth or glass fiber. Patterned fabrics are made with adequate color selections for a variety of installations. One textured Tontine®[1] glass shade cloth is manufactured in nine colors:

Bright White	Pongee
Pineapple	Red Hibscus
Sun Yellow	Caribbean Blue
Tropic Lime	Coconut Brown
Creamy Apricot	

Another variation is a cloth of vinyl-coated Fiberglas yarns woven in an open pattern which does not block the outside view but reduces solar heat penetration and effects cooling, reducing air-conditioning costs on exposed windows.[2]

There are infinite variations in window shade installations and trim. The basic considerations are whether the material should be opaque or translucent and whether flame resistance is a factor. Once the material is decided upon, the possibilities are endless. Shades may be trimmed with braid or fringe, or hemmed with special stitching. They may be installed with or without a valance, made to draw up or down, or reversed.

For special effect, fabric can be laminated to shade cloth. Present adhesives make lamination possible with a lasting bond. Tightly woven cottons, rayons, and linen fabrics produce the best results. While wallpaper can be used this way also, it does not stand up to hard wear, and the paper tends to buckle and crack with use. However, appliqués of the wallpaper pattern can be applied to the lower portion of the shade with good results. Original designs can also be painted on shade cloth.

A combination of pull-up and bottom-up shades in Pompeian brown with black braid trim not only affords complete privacy, but also acts as a beautiful background for furniture and flooring. These colors were selected from a magnificent Coromandel screen.

Whatever means are used to control light, they will affect the temperature of the room and will minimize fading of carpets, wall coverings, furniture, wood, etc. If there is a severe sun problem, special attention should be given to it before the final decision about light control is made.

The living room shown in Plate 29 is in rich browns and subtle beiges and takes its theme from the Portuguese rug. The window shade is laminated with a fabric in a black and brown flame-stitch pattern. The walls are mocha, providing a fitting background for the print collection and beige sofa. Accent is supplied

[1] Stauffer Chemical Co., Newburgh, NY 06880.

[2] Joanna Western Mills Company, Chicago, IL 60616.

FIG. 8.1 Executive Office
Virginia Frankel, A.S.I.D., Designer
Window Shade Manufacturers Association, New York, NY
Hilda D. Sachs

in the nasturtium covering of the armchair and the pillows. The careful use of black in the table, lamps, and other accessories adds to the sophistication of the room.

The contemporary office with tall windows and low window sills, Figure 8.1 was furnished with one group of pull-down shades to temper glare from above and another group installed bottom-up to lend privacy and soften light at eye level. The color scheme of red, white, and blue is carried out with white tie-back curtains trimmed with red braid. The shades are blueberry. Walnut bookshelves and desk, with white desk chair, are in quiet contrast to the conversation group of scarlet chairs and sofa in white surrounding the smoked-glass coffee table. The carpet is a houndstooth pattern of scarlet and blue.

An imaginative window treatment in a dining area employs an abstract sunburst pattern of pale gray, peach, and medium gray on a cloud gray canvas room-darkening shade, Figure 8.2. A medium gray border is painted at the bottom of the shade, which was installed reverse-roll to go all the way up and out of the way, or to act as a valance for the translucent shade installed behind the painted shade. The table acts as a divider between the dining area and the sun room.

An unusual use of shades was developed by a designer whose living room was predominantly off-white. A pair of handsome laminated window shades made from a baroque-stripe fabric in tangerine and off-white was the touchstone of the room scheme. Bottom-up shades on either side of the fireplace could be pulled up to introduce large areas of the same bold color. This provided a flexible use of pattern and color with little effort, and it formed the basis for a complete color scheme that included off-white ottomans, an off-white sofa with cushions of nasturtium, deep orange, and gold, and an area rug of geometric design in shades of rust, terra-cotta, black, and off-white.

Vertical blinds Vertical blinds are vanes or slats hung vertically rather than horizontally, and there are several different varieties on the market. An assortment of hardware allows the slats or vanes to be opened fully, tilted slightly, or closed, and in addition the blinds can be drawn to the side, as with curtains. Slats can be made of aluminum, fabric, or vinyl plastic and range in width from 3 to 4 inches. Color selections are wide. Over forty colors are available in vinyl vanes (Louvredrape), and custom effects can be obtained by combining accent-colored vanes with the main color, or by providing a shaded or striped effect. In addition, wallpaper can be applied to the vinyl slats.

Aluminum vertical-blind vanes are available in almost 100 different colors and patterns. The standard vane is 4 inches wide, and 3-inch or 3½-inch vanes can be obtained on special order.

Vertical-blind vanes can also be made using shade cloth, as in Plate 27, where the vanes are in a color called Spice; this provides good light control and imparts a contemporary feeling to the arched windows in an older house. The carpet is a muted red tweed, and the brick wall and fireplace have been left in their natural state. A neutral beige sofa, bright red chair, and red plastic tables framed with black or white tops complete the scheme.

In a studio apartment, Plate 28, vertical blinds of Breneman's textured space shade cloth are installed within mirrored lambrequins. The use of plum and white complements the modern abstract painting. The silver and white striated

FIG. 8.2   Dining Area
John Van Koert, Designer
Window Shade Manufacturers Association, New York, NY
Hilda D. Sachs

ceiling, silver-vinyl-covered campaign chests, and the sculpture of stainless steel combine to accent the entire scheme.

Roman shades Roman shades are among the most decorative means of controlling light. The suppliers of Roman shades are very design-conscious and can furnish a number of stock patterns as well as custom designs (Figures 8.3a–c). They are as decorative as wall hangings when in the closed position. One Mondrian-like abstract pattern of colored rug-weaving wool that contains short horizontal stripes is shown in the following colors on an off-white background: red orange and brown; brown; chartreuse and orange; chartreuse and brown; red; brown, yellow, and orange; green and orange; orange; and orange, green, and red.

PRINTS, PAINTINGS
AND PHOTOGRAPHS

The paintings, pictures, or sculpture used in a room will depend upon the taste of the client, the style of the architectural space in which they are to be used, and, of course, the suitability of color, pattern, and subject. Good art can be used in residences, offices, and public buildings. Whether they are originals or copies does not matter if they are properly selected and placed. Often the colors in a fine painting are the inspiration for the entire color scheme of a room or a series of architectural spaces.

The colors and intensities of a painting dictate the distance from which it should properly be viewed; this should be borne in mind when choosing and hanging it. Dimensions will depend upon many factors, such as the size and proportion of the available space. If the painting is large, its hues and intensities must be considered so that it is part of the room and not an isolated note. Fitness of subject matter should also be considered: one executive the author knows was chagrined to find that a semi-nude painting which he had hung in a conference room caused more discussion than the problems on the agenda. A large seascape with realistic waves in a doctor's reception room can cause some patients to become nauseated. Prints to be used in the psychiatric unit of a hospital should consist of peaceful landscapes in quiet colors; violent "motion" in a painting will sometimes cause violent reactions in a mentally ill person.

While some of the above considerations need not be regarded in residential work, other factors, such as architectural style, must be taken into account. An English period room will usually benefit by the use of narrative and disciplined art. Up to about the last quarter of the eighteenth century, a good English interior included only portraits, since other forms of painting were monopolized by the Italian and Flemish masters. The grand style of English portrait painting treated color with subtlety and restraint. For example, Sir Joshua Reynolds' (1723–1792) *Lady Elizabeth Delme and Her Children* (Mellon Collection, National Gallery of Art) contains soft shades of pink, blue, and white, with gray-brown trees and a low-key background which conveys dignity and good taste. Thomas Gainsborough's (1727–1788) *Portrait of Mrs. Richard Brinsley Sheridan* illustrates the same point. The lady's dress is a pastel pink; all colors around it, including those of the sky and trees, are soft gray green. In contrast, French portraits of this period frequently show the use of freer technique and bolder colors,

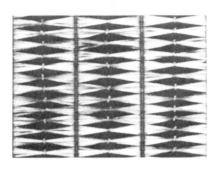

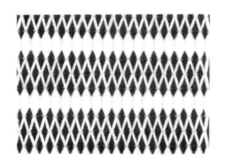

FIG. 8.3
Patterns of Roman Shades
(a) Hourglass
(b) Horizontal
(c) Lace
Window Modes, Inc., New York, NY

such as the bright yellow and terra-cotta in Jean Honoré Fragonard's (1732–1806) *A Young Girl Reading*.

A nineteenth-century English room often included still life paintings in natural colors—for example, bright red berries contrasted with a blue dish and silver bowl, all offset by a landscape in a window, as in John F. Francis's (1808–1886) still life *Strawberries and Cream*; or the naturalistic colors, deep and rich, of Winslow Homer's seascapes. In addition to oil paintings, nineteenth-century English rooms often included engravings, Audubon prints, and Currier and Ives prints, with color varying according to subject.

If the periods preceding the contemporary period were for the most part characterized by realism, it may be said that the comtemporary artist "expresses what he perceives; he perceives what he expresses."[3] In other words, if we remember that we see what we learn to see, that we see what we *want* to see, and that what we perceive is shaped by internal subjective factors as well as by external optical laws, then we can understand that the paintings which are used in architectural spaces can be successful without telling a story: they can be successful if they contain color and pattern which set the color tone for the area and if they contribute to it by their very size, shape, and placement.

In some modern art, objects are differentiated only by luminosity. If subject matter is disregarded, the quality of a painting can be judged by (among other things) how pleasing an abstract pattern it makes. In Henri Matisse's *Still Life with Goldfish* (1911), for instance, the importance lies in the place occupied by the objects and the empty spaces around them, i.e., proportion and composition.

Perhaps the most important difference between the art we term "modern" and that which preceded it is in the colors used. Colors suddenly become, as in Raoul Dufy's *The Artist and His Model in the Studio at Le Havre* (1929), brilliant light and dark blues, brilliant reds, orange, and pink. Compare this with the controlled impetuosity obtained by Paul Gauguin in his *The Moon and the Earth* (1893).

Otto Mueller in his *Gipsies with Sunflowers* (1927) used large areas of brilliant yellow and strong green. Louis Marcoussis, in *Two Poets* (1929), used a bright orange and green against a background of neutral colors.

But even within this period, there are differences in the way artists use color. In his *Composition with Red, Yellow and Blue* (1921), Piet Mondrian strategically placed relatively small amounts of blue, purple, orange, and yellow in a framework of black against a light background. Kazimir Malevich in his *Suprematist Composition* (1915) used red violet, blue violet, jade green, orange, and chinese red, as well as black and pink, in a disciplined and dynamic composition. Arshile Gorky, in *Agony* (1947), used bright shades of pink contrasted with spots of dark blue. Giuseppe Santomaso used brilliant deep yellow, oranges, and various shades of green on a bright yellow background in his composition entitled *Reds and Yellows of Harvest Time* (1957). Similarly, Ernst Wilhelm Nay in *Alpha* (1957) combines brilliant reds, blues, and greens in large patterns.

The colors used in many famous contemporary paintings inspire contem-

[3] Herbert Read, *A Concise History of Modern Painting*, New York: Frederick A. Praeger, Inc., 1959, p. 12.

porary interior color schemes. While pastel shades are often used today, they are usually employed as a foil for brilliant spots of color. Many architects and designers of contemporary interiors, inspired by the colors of modern paintings, use brilliant colors complemented by neutral tones (see Plate 28). For example, a putty sofa and red-orange chairs might be used in front of a pumpkin wall with a black and white painting on it; a putty sofa and emerald green chair in front of a spectrum-blue wall with a black and white print on it; or a black sofa and orange chairs in front of a spectrum-red wall with a painting in red, green, brown, and white. Just as often, bright red, orange, blue, green, or brown will be used in front of a white wall where the paintings are bright. To achieve quiet elegance, one may use deep brown furniture, a pumpkin carpet, and curtains of pale pumpkin or white. In such a room, a small bowl of yellow flowers will provide a superb accent; drawings or paintings should be muted. With black and white drawings or paintings, such as Picasso's *Four Ballet Dancers*, black and white are often used in parts of the room. "Op art," or "perceptual abstraction," uses both brilliant color and complex arrangements of black and white. Regardless of subject matter or period, black and white can usually be used successfully with spots of brilliant color (see Plate 29).

For those whose interest lies in photography, this medium offers broad possibilities for creative effects, whether the photos are the result of a hobby or purchased from a professional. Black and white photographs are always stunning, but advances in color photography offer additional ways to achieve variety.

The photomural has been available for many years in black and white, although occasionally such murals were hand colored. Recent technical developments have made it possible to produce large photographs resembling wall coverings from small camera-size photographic transparencies (see Figure 8.4). One firm produces murals on high-gloss paper and on several linen-like fabrics, as well as certain fine rayon and nylon fabrics. Other colored photomurals[4] have been mounted on Masonite, transferred to ceramic tiles, or used between Plexiglas panels.

ACCESSORIES

The successful selection of colorful accessories is not an accident. They cannot simply be selected at random if one hopes to complete and complement an otherwise integrated color scheme. The range of accessories available is so wide and so personal that it is possible in the space available here merely to establish guidelines. A sense of fitness is important. Personal taste is perhaps the most usual criterion for the selection of accessories, but the style of the room should be considered.

Those who design period rooms, if they are purists, select accessories which were popular during the respective periods in which they seek inspiration. Those who prefer antique accessories hunt constantly for rare, appropriate

[4] *Interior Design,* vol. 48, no. 3, March 1977, p. 126.

FIG. 8.4   Architecture Painting
           Created from a photograph by Ron Winch, St. Paul, MN
           3M Company, St. Paul, MN

pieces. For instances, if one is designing in the Colonial style, accessories might include tall case clocks, pewter, kitchenware, pictures and maps, firearms, and lanterns. If the objects are authentic, the colors will be correct. If one is doing a room in the style of the early eighteenth century, one might include Oriental china and English staffordshire, wedgwood, chelsea, and derby, as well as sandwich-glass items. On the other hand, if the room is eighteenth-century French, crystal chandeliers, wall brackets, mirrors, Sèvres porcelain, and marble busts are appropriate. Designers who prefer to blend more than one style in a room have their choice of accessories from the styles being combined. It is perfectly acceptable to use a small number of antique accessories in a contemporary room. A group of engravings or prints made centuries ago will usually add charm to a contemporary room if subject matter is appropriate, the size is correct, and the grouping and placing are attractive.

Thanks to the excellence of commercial exchange, rare accessories may now be obtained with relative ease. While the world traveler enjoys the thrill of discovering rare accessories, he or she soon finds that many are available at home, where they may be selected at leisure for color and appropriateness. However, the truly rare items a traveler discovers abroad are the things likely to be enjoyed most. Imagine the anticipation with which the captains of New England clipper ships were greeted when they returned from the Orient with silk, tea chests, screens, and canton china!

As emphasized earlier, the colors of accessories must relate to the general color scheme of a room (see Plates 46, 156, 20, and 29). They should contribute to and be enhanced by it. A chinese red Oriental chest will contribute only if it harmonizes or complements the total color scheme, and if the chinese red is repeated elsewhere in the room. A green bowl with yellow chrysanthemums will look good in a white and yellow room with a pale green carpet. Objects of natural-finished wood will look good almost anywhere. Copper kitchen utensils and orange-brown natural-baked clay pots will be attractive in a kitchen-dining area where warm tones of orange and off-white are used on walls and floor. A curry-yellow porcelain bowl on a black base will key an entire room of yellow, green, and white if it is placed strategically. A brass filigreed jewel box will be quite at home in a room where the colors are predominantly warm; the same type of box made of silver or pewter will add a great deal to a room which is cool in color.

From the above it may be seen that the color of accessories must contribute to the room, and the room must contribute to the accessories.

The colors one uses will depend upon the job at hand: a bright and happy room calls for rich, deep accessories. A subdued room, in which all of the colors are, say, restful grays and browns, will be enhanced by bright accessories.

No interior is complete without plants, flowers, or both. If possible, the beauties of an exterior garden should be continued inside by means of large glass areas. If not, plants or flowers can be artfully placed in at least the most important rooms to accentuate their colors. Flowers may be placed in glass or pottery vases whose colors complement those of the flowers and the room. A vase of pale yellow roses will look good in a yellow-green room, pink roses in a pink and blue room, pale greenish-white dogwood in a yellow, green, and orange room, and red, purple, and white flowers in a blue and white room.

Yellow-hearted daisies will always enhance a black and white room. Green plants or vases of green leaves will harmonize with almost any color scheme.

The number of accessories should be limited, or clutter will result. As accessories are usually small and easily moved, seasonal changes may be made. If a collection of items is to be displayed, a special cupboard or cabinet probably will enhance its effectiveness.

LAMPS

Although modern architectural lighting for the most part precludes the use of lamps, they can be used to advantage if their size, color, and shape are determined in the initial study of an architectural space. While those for reading differ in size and color from those used for general light, all lamps in an area should have certain similarities. For instance, the inside reflecting surface of lampshades should be white, and there should be no direct transmitted reflected glare. The lamps should contribute to the room's general illumination by providing a generous amount of upward light. The bulb in a lamp should be located as low as possible so as to spread light over a wide area, but it should not, of course, be visible from a sitting position. Floor lamps should be located behind the user to protect his or her eyes from direct glare.

The materials for lamps will vary according to the period of the room in which they are to be used. Materials for lamps to be used in traditional rooms are most appropriate if they reflect the materials and are compatible with the artifacts of that period. An Early American room, for instance, may have lamps of brass, pewter, copper, wood, or pottery; those in a contemporary room might be made of any of these, or of stainless steel, chromed metal, ceramics, enamelware, plastic, marble, crystal, leather, iron, or wood. The wood may be used alone or in combination with other materials—for example, brass. A material, traditional or otherwise, is acceptable if it harmonizes with the colors of the room and if it is appropriate in form and size.

The lamp's base and shade colors, and its scale as well, must fit the total design. In many cases, when the bases of the lamps are of a material that can be painted, colors which complement or harmonize with the rest of the room are used.

The color of the shade and its trim must be selected to harmonize with the base, and the shade material itself must be appropriate in texture. An off-white with a yellowish overtone may be acceptable in a yellow room, while a bluish-white will be appropriate in a blue or green room. The material used for shades can be silk (taffeta or shantung), paper, grasscloth, or plastic. All of these are available in many colors. A lamp must be considered as a piece of sculpture, and its shape, form, and color must be treated as integral parts of the total three-dimensional composition in which it is to be used.

CONCLUSION

From the foregoing description of materials, furniture, and furnishings, one may see that the number of available colors is almost unlimited. At no other time in the history of the world have so many hues, tints, and shades been so widely available. No longer is the choice of color limited to the chief of state, the clergy, or the wealthy. Color has truly become a universal property.

But the very freedom presented by this universality imposes responsibilities. We may use color as we wish, only if it does not adversely affect those around us.

In any case, it is certain that this freedom will continue to increase. New hues are appearing every day; travelers will continue to carry colors and color combinations from one part of the world to another. Architectural styles will be developed to meet the technological and social challenges that will occur in our world, and the color requirements for these new forms will be studied by architects and interior designers. These professionals will develop guidelines for their use.

Manufacturers will continue to diversify; chemists and physicists will develop new products in new colors. Methods of lighting will change. Out of the raw materials provided by technicians, the architect and interior designer will continue to provide leadership in the development and use of color for architectural spaces which will be functional, appropriate, and elegant.

All who are engaged in the design of interiors will agree that successful interior design is dependent upon long and careful training and a thorough knowledge of materials and their potential. While color in itself occupies an important position in the design of an interior, it cannot, of course, be used apart from texture, scale, proportion, and form. Guides for the use of color should be mastered. But in the end the success of a color scheme will depend not only upon the color designer's theoretical knowledge but also upon his or her natural ability and taste, and on a certain amount of inspiration and emotion.

BIBLIOGRAPHY

AIA Honor Award 1949–1961, *Mid Century Architecture in America,* edited and with an Introduction by Wolf von Eckart, Foreword by Philip Will, Jr., F.A.I.A., Baltimore: The Johns Hopkins Press, 1961.

Albers, Josef, *Interaction of Color,* New Haven: Yale University Press, 1963.

American Carpet Institute, Inc., four sales manuals, New York.

Arms, Brock, A.I.A., A.I.D., N.S.I.D., "Interiors: What Is the Architect's Role?" The Octagon, Washington, D.C., *AIA Journal,* Dec. 1966.

Baker, Hollis, *Furniture in the Ancient World,* New York: The Macmillan Company: 1966.

Birren, Faber, *Color in Interiors: Historical and Modern,* New York: Whitney Library of Design, 1963.

————, *New Horizons in Color,* New York: Reinhold Publishing Corporation, 1955.

Boger, H. Batterson, *The Traditional Art of Japan,* Garden City, N.Y.: Doubleday & Company, Inc., 1964.

Burnham, R. W., R. M. Hanes, and C. J. Bartelson, *Color: A guide to Basic Facts and Concepts,* New York: John Wiley & Sons, Inc., 1963.

Burris, Meyer E., *Color Design in the Decorative Arts,* Englewood Cliffs, N.J.: Prentice-Hall, Inc., 1945.

————, *Contemporary Color Guide,* New York: William Helburn, Inc., 1947.

Campbell, Gordon, and I. O. Evans, *The Book of Flags,* 6th ed., London: Oxford University Press, 1969.

Ciba Review, 1962/1-6: Published by Ciba Ltd., Basel, Switzerland. Represented in the United States by Ciba Chemical and Dye Company (Division of Ciba Corp.), Fair Lawn, N.J. See vol. 4, p. 30.

Ciba Review, Vols. 1–24, Sept. 1937 to Aug. 1939.

Ciba Review, Vol. 1, 1963, pp. 11–22.

Commery, E. W., and C. Eugene Stephenson, *How to Decorate and Light Your Home,* New York: Coward-McCann, Inc., 1955.

Cooke, H. L. (Curator), *British Painting in the National Gallery of Art,* Washington, D.C.: Publications Fund, National Gallery of Art, 1960.

————, *French Painting of the Sixteenth and Eighteenth Centuries in the National Gallery of Art,* Washington, D.C.: Publications Fund, National Gallery of Art, 1959.

Dantyagi, Susheela, *Fundamentals of Textiles and Their Care,* Bombay: Orient Longmans, Ltd., 1964.

Denny, Grace Goldena, *Fabrics and How to Know Them,* Philadelphia: J. B. Lippincott Company, 1923.

The Development of Various Decorative and Upholstery Fabrics, New York: F. Schumacher & Co., 1924.

Eberlein, H. D., and A. E. Richardson, *The English Inn, Past and Present,* Philadelphia & London: J. P. Lippincott Company, 1926.

Encyclopedia of Textiles, American Fabrics Magazine (ed.)., Englewood Cliffs, N.J.: Prentice-Hall, Inc., 1960.

Evans, Ralph, M., *An Introduction to Color,* New York: John Wiley & Sons, Inc., 1948.

Facts About Contract Carpeting, The International Wool Secretariat, Carpet Marketing Dept., Wool House, Carlton Gardens, London, SWIY 5 AE, Nov. 1975.

Fletcher, Sir Bannister, *A History of Architecture on the Comparative Method,* New York: Charles Scribner's Sons, 1928.

Focillan, Henri, *The Art of the West in the Middle Ages, Vol. 1, Romanesque Art,* London: Phaidon Press, Ltd., 1963.

Gardner, Helen, *Art through the Ages,* revised by Horst de la Croix & Richard G. Tansey, New York: Harcourt Brace Jovanovich, 1970.

Glazier, Richard, *Historic Textile Fabrics,* New York: Charles Scribner's Sons, 1923.

Graves, Maitland, *Color Fundamentals,* New York: McGraw-Hill Book Company, 1952.

"Great Beginnings" Pamphlet, Bigelow-Sanford, Inc., New York, 1969.

Hamilton, Edward A., *Graphic Design for the Computer Age,* New York: Van Nostrand-Reinhold Company, 1970.

Hardwood Plywood Manufacturers Association, *Versatile Hardwood Plywood,* Arlington, Va.: 1966.

House & Garden, *The Modern Interior,* Robert Harling (ed.), London: Vogue House, Hanover Square, and The Condé Nast Publications, Ltd., 1964.

Huntington, W. C., *Building Construction,* 3d ed., New York: John Wiley & Sons, Inc., 1963.

Illuminating Engineering Society, *IES Lighting Handbook,* 5th ed., New York: 1972.

Inter-Society Color Council, *Inter Chem: The Story of Color and Demonstration in Color Perception,* Interchemical Corp., 1965.

Jacobson, Egbert, *Basic Color: An Interpretation of the Ostwald Color System,* Chicago: Paul Theobald & Company, 1948.

———, *Trademark Design,* Chicago: Paul Theobald & Company, 1952.

Judd, Deane B., *Color in Our Daily Lives,* U.S. Dept. of Commerce, National Bureau of Standards, Consumer Information Series 6, March 1975.

Kelly, Kenneth L., "A Universal Color Language" (reprint), *Color Engineering,* vol. 3, no. 2, March/April 1965.

Ketchum, Howard, *Color Planning for Business and Industry,* New York: Harper & Row, Publishers, Inc., 1958.

Koblo, Martin, *World of Color,* New York: McGraw-Hill Book Company, 1962.

Koch, Robert, *Louis Tiffany, Rebel in Glass,* New York: Crown Publishers, Inc., 1964.

Küpper, Harald, *Color: Origin, Systems, Uses,* translated by F. Bradley, London: Van Nostrand-Reinhold, Ltd., 1972.

Lowry, Bates, *The Visual Experience: An Introduction to Art,* New York: Harry N. Abrams, Inc., and Englewood Cliffs, N.J.: Prentice-Hall, Inc., 1964.

Lynes, Russell, *The Tastemakers,* New York: Harper & Row, Publishers, Incorporated, 1949, 1953, 1954.

Maas, James B., Jill K. Jayson, and Douglas A. Kleiber, "Effects of Spectral Differences in Illumination on Fatigue," *Journal of Applied Psychology,* vol. 59, no. 4, 1974, pp. 524–526.

Malkin, Jane, "Psychological, Emotional Factors Guide Health-Care Facility Design," *Contract,* Feb. 1976.

Morse, Edward S., *Japanese Homes and Their Surroundings,* New York: Dover Publications, Inc., 1961 (orig. 1886).

Munsell, A. H., *A Color Notation* (A measured color system, based on the three qualities hue, value and chroma, with illustrative models, charts, and a course of study arranged for teachers), 2d ed., Boston: George H. Ellis Co., 1907.

Parker, Harry, C. M. Gay, and J. W. MacGuire, *Materials and Methods of Architectural Construction,* 3d ed., New York: John Wiley & Sons, Inc., 1958.

Reade, Herbert, *A Concise History of Modern Painting,* New York: Frederick A. Praeger, Inc., 1959.

Rorimer, James J., *The Cloisters,* New York: The Metropolitan Museum of Art, 1939.

Schlumberger, Eveline, "The Case of the Ambierle Altarpiece," *Réalités,* July 1965.

Seitz, William C., *The Responsive Eye,* New York: The Museum of Modern Art, 1965.

Sellars, R. W., *The Essentials of Logic,* Boston: Houghton Mifflin Company, 1925.

Smith, Bradley, *Japan: A History in Art,* New York: Simon & Schuster, Inc., 1964.

Stenico, Arturo, *Roman and Etruscan Painting,* New York: The Viking Press, Inc., 1963.

Styne, Alexander, F., Chairman, "Report of the Subcommittee for Problem 33: Human Response to Color," *Inter-Society Color Council Newsletter,* Annual Report Issue, No. 242, May-June 1976, pp. 13–14.

Terry, Charles S., *Masterworks of Japanese Art,* Rutland, Vt., and Tokyo, Japan: Charles E. Tuttle Co., 1956.

Thorington, L., F.I.E.S., L. Parascandola, and Lynn Cunningham, "Visual and Biologic Aspects of an Artificial Sunlight Illuminant," *Journal of Illuminating Engineering Society,* Oct. 1971, p. 33.

——, "Light, Biology and People," Lighting Design and Application, *The Illuminating Engineering Society,* 1974.

Tile Council of America, Inc., *Recommended Standard Specifications for Ceramic Tile,* TCA 137.1, 1976.

Tokyo National Museum, *100 Masterpieces from the Collection,* Tokyo: 1959.

Whitney, F. L., *The Elements of Research,* Englewood Cliffs, N.J.: Prentice-Hall, Inc., 1942.

Whiton, Sherrill, *The Elements of Interior Decoration,* Philadelphia J. B. Lippincott Company, 1944.

Woldering, Irmgard, *The Art of Egypt—The Time of the Pharaohs,* translated by Anne E. Keep, New York: Crown Publishers, Inc., 1963.

Wright, Frank Lloyd, *The Natural House,* New York: Horizon Press, 1954.

Wurtman, Richard J., "The Effects of Light on the Human Body," *Scientific American,* vol. 233, no. 1, July 1975, pp. 68–77.

INDEX